FUN & GAMES
for
FAMILY GATHERINGS
with a FOCUS on REUNIONS

First Edition

Adrienne E. Anderson

REUNION RESEARCH • SAN FRANCISCO • CALIFORNIA

Cover design by Diana Stewart
Illustrations by Kathy Clo
Book design by Tom Ninkovich

Published by:

> Reunion Research
> 3145 Geary Blvd #14
> San Francisco, CA 94118

Distributed by:

> Betterway Books, an imprint of F&W Publications
> 1507 Dana Ave.
> Cincinnati, OH 45207

Printed in Canada

Library of Congress Cataloging in Publication Data:

Anderson, Adrienne E.

Fun & games for family gatherings: with a focus on reunions/
Adrienne E. Anderson. – 1st ed.
p. cm.

Includes index.
ISBN 0-9610470-5-4

1. Family recreation. 2. Games. 3. Family reunions. I. Title

GV182.8.A53   1995
790.1'91–dc20   95-41090
                                              CIP

—DEDICATION—

In MEMORY of

My Mother
Caroline Maude Chancellor
Who taught me how to laugh,

and

My Husband
Carl William Anderson, Jr.
Who loved to plan parties.

SOURCES and ACKNOWLEDGEMENTS

Solomon of old proclaimed, "There is nothing new under the sun." Many of the games we play today have been transmitted through the centuries from generation to generation. Innumerable influences have added new variations. So it is that many of the ideas proposed in this book have unknown roots.

My husband and I have been collecting game ideas for over forty years—often scribbled on a scrap of paper or on the back of an envelope—a brainwave for a new twist discussed, and eventually transferred to a shoebox card file which grew to two and beyond. For this reason we often cannot acknowledge a source. Where a source is known, it has been acknowledged and written permission has been granted for inclusion in this collection. If I have inadvertently included material whose source should have been acknowledged, I beg indulgence. Should such be brought to my attention, I will do my best to correct this in future editions.

A special thanks to our former college students who allowed us to use them as "guinea pigs" for experimentation at our parties and reunions, and who also contributed their own ideas to our fund of fun things to do; to my granddaughter, Alida Anderson, who came up with some great games of her own; and to my editor, Tom Ninkovich.

Adrienne Anderson

Alberta, Canada

The twentieth century has seen a whole new society come into being. In all preceeding centuries, the family, the community, and the church were the center of all social life. With the advent of technology came a new mobility and choice of lifestyles. People were removed from their roots. Many people presently feel disconnected from their past.

Perhaps this is why there is a movement to foster family gatherings and other opportunities for people to "connect," such as through club and camp experiences—interacting with people of similar needs. Some families may get together to celebrate holidays such as Christmas, New Years or Memorial Day. Others celebrate milestones such as graduations, birthdays, anniversaries, and births. Some religions observe a "Family Night" once a week or once a month. And let's not forget the Family Reunion, which was the original influence for my collecting the information for this book. These gatherings all give us a sense of who we are and from whence we come. It's important to keep in mind their purpose—to foster growing relationships.

These events may last a few hours, a day, a weekend or (in the case of some reunions) a week. They may be once-in-a-lifetime events (such as a 50th wedding anniversary) or they may be old family traditions (one family I know of has held an annual reunion for over fifty years).

The time frame you have to work with will be a determining factor in your planning. A one-day gathering can feature only a few events. Examples might be an auction, a hobby display, or a quick game or two. A weekend can have several major features, e.g. longer games, family stories and history, a banquet with entertainment. However, some gatherings may attract people from all parts of the globe and last several days. At such events, older people will delight in visiting and reminiscing, but special activities should be planned for the younger generations to capture their interest. Consider some of the nature crafts (which can also involve all ages) and some of the special outings and games for teens.

There are many "how-to" books for planning family gatherings of various sorts. This volume is designed rather to suggest "what-to-do." It is intended to be an idea file. Hopefully, there will be something in it that will be useful to you and your unique situation or will help spark your own ingenuity.

Ideas for family gatherings are endless. If you have a good idea for family activities or games, I would be delighted to hear from you and include your suggestions in the next edition of this book.

Have a fun-filled get-together!!!

A. E. A.

TABLE of CONTENTS

Chapter 1

A POTPOURRI of FAMILY REUNION IDEAS

Reunions are perhaps the most popular family gathering, and most of them require some advanced planning. Here are some specific ideas to help with organizing your next reunion. Read all the way through and mark those ideas you think would be particularly useful for your situation. Also check Appendix C for resources.

Registration

✓ (#1) If you expect a large crowd and must have a formal registration, speed the process by having separate stations for each family branch or surname (if there are enough different surnames to make this category useful). Allocate as many tables or stations as you think necessary and have them designated by signs marked clearly with the branch names of the family, or alphabetically with A–G, H–M, etc. Tables can be color-coded to match family branches (see Name Tags).

✓ (#2) At each registration table have 3x5 file cards with the head of each household written in the upper right corner of the card. These are to be filled in with current address, phone number, and other pertinent information as the person registers. These either become your permanent file or are used to update and verify an already existing file. If you expect to use these cards to compile a family directory, then information on children, birthdates, anniversaries, etc, should also be included. File cards come in at least seven colors, and could easily be color-coded to represent various branch lines. Or small, colored, self-stick dots could be applied to an upper corner of the cards. These dots are available at all stationery stores. See Appendix C for sources.

✓ (#3) Have Family Group Sheets at your registration table (see Appendix B). Before the gathering, someone could fill in as much information as is available. Then at the reunion ask family members to add further information or make corrections. You will be more apt to have them completed if the job is not too tedious.

✓ (#4) Make up "Goody Bags"—one for each family, to be given out at registration. Commercial firms or Convention and Visitors Bureaus might be contacted for note pads, advertising pens, pencils, fridge magnets, local give-away items, even the bags themselves.

✓ (#5) Guessing contests are always fun. Set up a table with pads of paper, pencils and a box for guesses. Jelly beans in a jar are a popular item, but you might come up with an original idea that would be indicative of your family. Using pennies will simplify the counting process because they come in rolls of 50 from the bank.

Name Tags

✓ (#6) For unique name tags, ahead of time prepare squares of construction paper of different colors cut approximately 3"x 4". Have each person *tear* a shape that tells something about themselves or indicates a hobby; for example, a flower for someone who enjoys gardening. You will be surprised at the innovative ideas people will have. The name tags become good conversation starters if you have a large group with many people who have not met before. They could also be used as a mixer where people try to guess what the shapes represent. Or use your imagination to dream up other uses. Provide *wide-tipped* marking pens so names can be clearly read. Nothing is more frustrating than trying to peer at illegible name tags.

✓ (#7) Another good idea is to color-code name tags for particular branches of families. If great-grandma and great-grandpa had nine children, have a different color for each family branch. Have a color chart posted on a wall that identifies the various branches. Personalized T-shirts can be color coded, too.

BROWN FAMILY REUNION

FAMILY TREE and
NAME TAG DISPENSER.

✓ (#8) Name tags can be numbered to be used later in a drawing.

✓ (#9) Two or three name tags have *duplicate numbers*. Anyone finding another name tag with the same number is entitled to a prize.

Memorabilia

✓ (#10) When you mail out the reunion announcements, ask family members to bring copies of obituaries, immigration and naturalization papers, graduation announcements, newspaper articles, pictures, etc. You might ask for copies rather than originals if you do not want to be responsible for loss of important memorabilia. Have someone prepared to go to a photocopy machine to make copies for the family historian or genealogist—or rent or borrow a copy machine.

✓ (#11) Have an exhibit of family artifacts: a fan from "the old country," great-grandpa's glasses, a branding iron, etc.

✓ (#12) Start a reunion scrapbook with pictures and memorabilia taken at the reunion. Pass this along at the end of the reunion to the person responsible to plan the next one, and display at each succeeding reunion.

✓ (#13) If your gathering is indoors, prepare an attractive bulletin board and/or table where anyone can post anything they like in the way of memorabilia. If you expect they might have items they wouldn't want tack holes in, have clear mylar sleeves available. Encourage people to bring pictures of family members who cannot be present, or pictures of weddings and graduations that have occurred since the last reunion.

✓ (#14) If you are *really* ambitious, you might prepare a bulletin board for each family line with colored edging to match other color-coded features. This makes it easy to identify what has been happening in each separate branch of the family.

Photography/Videography

✓ (#15) Have a photographic display. Make a game—mix photos and names to be matched.

✓ (#16) Have a photography contest. A limited number of entries (e.g. three per person) might be a guideline. Have an impartial judge, perhaps from outside the family, who would be willing to come and judge at a particular time. Offer prizes.

✓ (#17) Hire a professional photographer to take a group picture and also group pictures of family branches, first cousins, etc.

✓ (#18) Have a family reunion video made: groups, exhibits, activities. Copies may be ordered. (See Appendix A.)

✓ (#19) If you are near a 1-hour film processing store, arrange for a photo display as soon as possible. Take group photos of each generation and take orders for prints.

✓ (#20) Have each family bring a *very* limited (5 per family?) number of slides with a brief written explanation accompanying them. Be sure they are marked with the name of the owner. Appoint a skillful co-ordinator who will put together a slide presentation and return the slides to the donors. This way Uncle Bertram won't be able to monopolize with interminable accounts of his exploits!

✓ (#21) Mark the family name lightly on a large field (use baking flour). Have people stand on the marks to spell out the family name for a photo. This must be taken from a high vantage point.

✓ (#22) If the group is not large enough to spell out the family name, have the kids and teens lie on the ground to spell out the letters using their bodies! Stand on a rooftop to take the picture.

✓ (#23) Make large placards (bristol board comes in 22"x28" size) with one letter of the family name on each card. Take a group photo with the front row holding the placards. Use later to make Christmas cards, postcards or just send prints to each family attending. If the reunion is an annual event, also make a card with the date. Store the placards, and take a new photo each year, revising the date. Use as a title page for each year in your family reunion scrapbook.

✓ (#24) Have a group photograph made. Then order photo Christmas cards by the packet to sell to family members in the fall.

✓ (#25) While people are visiting, have someone wandering with a tape recorder to catch snatches of conversations. Keep it brief. Seven minutes total recording time is probably enough. Play as a feature at the banquet.

Fund-raising

✓ (#26) Have a "White Elephant" sale. One person's junk is another person's treasure. Proceeds go toward funding future reunions, a newsletter or a family scholarship.

✓ (#27) Have a raffle. Does anyone have quilt-making skills or do you have an artist in the family who could do up a nice family tree?

✓ (#28) Have a craft table and sale.

✓ (#29) Bake sales are always popular. What woman doesn't like to sample another's specialty? Unless it is a family secret, items might be sold with the recipe attached. If it have been passed down for generations, the story might also be attached.

✓ (#30) Appoint someone to gather family recipes to be compiled and sold at the next reunion. See Appendix C for companies that print personalized cook books.

✓ (#31) Feature a toy and game exchange. Toys and games outgrown by one family might be welcomed by another. A nominal charge might be made to benefit future reunions.

✓ (#32) Have a used book or record/tape exchange or sale.

✓ (#33) Have an auction. Feature an oil painting of the original homestead painted by a talented family member or a professional. The auction could be the last major feature of the reunion. Proceeds are donated to the family reunion fund.

✓ (#34) Make and sell postcards. This might be a sketch or photo of the original homestead, a picture of the home or area from which they emigrated, or a photograph of the emigrant progenitors.

✓ (#35) Commission an artist to do a pen and ink sketch from photos of the family homestead. Create a limited edition set of 16"x18" prints to be sold at the family reunion. As this would be a little more costly than postcards, T-shirts or other keepsakes, it should be previously announced by mail.

✓ (#36) Arrange to have family pins made to sell at the reunion. Good discounts can usually be obtained if you order at least 75.

✓ (#37) Order blank photo calendars to make up your own family calendar to sell. See Appendix C for sources.

✓ (#38) A family store: A concession where popcorn, poppycock, sodas, candied apples and other snacks are sold. Also, imprinted items like T-shirts, pens, caps, etc.

✓ (#39) Grab bag/surprise bags—all kinds of donated articles are wrapped and placed on a table, put in a barrel, or wheeled around in a decorated cart. Both adults and children can purchase a bag for a small amount. They could be color-coded for men, women, boys, girls—or let them take their chances!

✓ (#40) Haggle table—a variation of "White Elephants." Have a sign stating that nothing is priced, make an offer. Buyer makes an offer, seller tries to up the price.

✓ (#41) Most people like tote-bags for various uses. Have a seamstress in your clan make tote-bags to sell. Encourage her to experiment with different fabrics, designs, miscellaneous pockets for different purposes. Sell at a special table at the craft sale.

Other Features

✓ (#42) Awards: Prizes might be awarded for any or all of the following:

1. Oldest person present
2. Couple married the longest
3. Newest married couple
4. Largest single family unit with all present
5. Person with most descendants present
6. Youngest person present
7. Person who traveled farthest to attend the reunion
8. If it is a regular event, person who has attended the most reunions
9. Oldest twins present, or any twins present

✓ (#43) Have a hobby display area. Many people have interesting avocations—they may even find another family member with a similar bent. Woodcarving, stamps, coins, model trains; collections of many kinds might be featured.

✓ (#44) For an ice-breaker, particularly for adults, gather baby pictures of those you expect to attend, or have people bring them. Mount them on cardstock or construction paper and number them. Give a sheet of paper to each participant with corresponding numbers listed. Have them guess who's who. Have a prize for the person with the most correct guesses. *Variation:* Have slides made from prints, and have a slideshow as a feature at the potluck supper or banquet. Be sure you have arranged for adequate equipment: screen or white sheet if there is no suitable wall space that they may be projected on, sufficient extension cords, extra bulb, etc.

✓ (#45) If you have family members too infirm or handicapped to attend, make a collage of reunion pictures, ribbons and other memorabilia to send them. Or have a roll of white shelf paper and colored marking pens available. Let those at the reunion write messages, make sketches or give brief descriptions of some of the events at the reunion.

✔ (#46) Gather pictures and have someone compile a family story-book for the young 'uns. These can be reproduced on a good photocopy machine.

✔ (#47) Have all the descendants of each family line stand together to be identified. Have a special recognition of the family branch with the most people in attendance. Take photos and videos.

✔ (#48) If yours is a large reunion, consider renting a school dorm during summer or Christmas break. They often have kitchen facilities, and you might make use of the gym for activities in case the weather doesn't co-operate. See *Budget Lodging Guide* in Appendix C.

Ethnic Ideas

✔ (#49) Feature your national heritage. Have a large banner with the family name and flag of the country of origin, with dates of reunions that have been held inscribed all around the borders. Have everyone sign it.

PIÑATA

✔ (#50) Use flags, tablecloths and table settings in national colors and motifs (e.g. red, white and green for Mexican heritage). See Appendix C for sources.

✔ (#51) One family of Swedish heritage had a children's choir of descendants dressed in Swedish costumes. They sang folk songs and hymns in both Swedish and English.

✔ (#52) Always encourage ethnic food at potlucks.

For Future Organization

✔ (#53) Keep a 3-ring notebook detailing arrangements made, number attending, special features, costs, mistakes, etc. If there were items that should be improved (e.g. registration bottlenecks, not enough visiting time allotted, not enough help, etc.), pass this information on to those responsible for co-ordinating future reunions. Also include address lists, phone numbers, committees, etc.

✓ (#54) Use the opportunity of the reunion to select a family historian, genealogist, and/or a representative from each branch of the family. A teen representative (or two) is also a good idea, especially to increase overall teen interest and attendance. The family genealogist or historian is in charge of Family Group Sheets (see Appendix B), biographies, clippings, copies of pertinent certificates, photographs, scrapbooks, and any memorabilia they wish to collect. The family representative could be responsible for gathering information on her branch of the family, keeping the genealogist or historian updated on family information (births, deaths, special occasions) and be a liaison to inform branch members about gatherings, etc.

✓ (#55) If you do not anticipate more than one reunion or are uncertain if another will be planned, it might be a good idea when people are all together to discuss the possibility of starting a family newsletter. Even if it is printed and distributed only once a year, it would keep new-found relatives in touch. It would also be an excellent starting point if another reunion were planned even in the distant future. It might be necessary to have a raffle or take up a collection to have the funds to get a newsletter off the ground. (See "Fund-raising" in this chapter.)

See page 128 for a description of *Family Reunion Handbook*, a very thorough book on planning family reunions.

Teddy Bear's
Picnic, #59

Chapter 2

GAMES for PRE-SCHOOLERS

If your gathering is held outdoors, young children will enjoy the freedom to run around. However, you might want some planned activities to give parents a break. Several people with a special affinity for little people might be assigned to plan pre-school activities. Don't lose sight of the fact that one of the goals is togetherness.

Play Characteristics of Pre-Schoolers

Understanding a bit about the play characteristics of young children might circumvent potential problems. Be aware that:

1. Two- and three-year-olds generally play independently but side by side. They are egocentric and may not want to share. As this is normal behavior, plan for each child to "do his own thing." Don't force cooperative play at this age.

2. Four- and five-year-olds may begin to play co-operatively but may not stick with one activity for very long.

*   *   *   *   *

The following activities are listed roughly by order of ascending complexity.

Nature Walk (#56)

Plan a simple nature walk where each child tries to find the prettiest stone, largest leaf, a wild flower, etc. Give each child a small "treasure bag" where they may store their "finds" to show Mom and Dad upon returning.

Play Dough (#57)

Prepare and have on hand: homemade play dough, individual styrofoam meat trays or plastic sheets for each child to work on, and shapes such as cookie cutters to work with.

Recipe for homemade play dough (no cooking, no refrigeration):

2 1/2 c. flour	2 c. boiling water
1/2 c. salt	Food coloring
1 Tbsp. alum	3 Tbsp. cooking oil; add one Tbsp. at a time.

Combine flour, salt and alum. Add the rest of the ingredients. Mix, using rubber gloves. Begin to knead as soon as possible and knead for a few minutes. Store in covered containers. Makes four cups.

Face Painting (#58)

A popular activity for children. Obtain painting kits from a costume or art store. Teenagers are often very good at painting faces.

Teddy Bear's Picnic (#59)

Plan a "Teddy Bear's Picnic." Great for 2–5 year olds. Take an old blanket and a few extra stuffed toys in the event that some child has not brought a stuffed companion. Mention the event in mailed announcements and ask parents to encourage the child to take a favorite stuffed toy from home. Have simple snacks.

Plastic cups with lids and straws, often found at fast-food places, will result in fewer "accidents." Ritz Bits Sandwiches filled with peanut butter make easy finger food. For entertainment, bring equipment for bubble blowing (a great outdoor activity!) and take a simple book with large pictures to be read—preferably featuring teddy bears or a nature story. A nice added touch would be to play a tape recording of "The Teddy Bear's Picnic." *Hint:* to make bubbles that last longer, add a few drops of cooking oil to the soap and water mixture.

Follow the Leader (#60)

Set the pace for children by hopping, walking, running, waving arms in airplane fashion, tooting on trumpets, etc. Children may take turns being the leader, but change frequently.

Balloons (#61)

Have lots of balloons—more than one per child, as inevitably some will be broken. Plan balloon tossing contests or a simple race kicking balloons along the ground toward a goal. *Please refer to our complete chapter on balloon games (Chapter 8).*

Jellybean Exchange (#62)

Give each child a ziploc bag or small basket with a dozen or more jellybeans of different colors. Set a time limit and let the children go about exchanging with one another. Each child is to try to get as many jellybeans of one color as she wishes in her container. She must decide which color she wants, then seek someone who is seeking another color and exchange with him. They all win—they all get to eat their own collection of jellybeans!

Egg Hunt (#63)

Inexpensive plastic eggs can be purchased and filled with candy or small favors and toys. You might have people collecting small toys from cereal boxes, etc, for the months before. While the children's attention is focused elsewhere, hide these objects all over the grounds. Be sure you have *lots* of them. You don't want any child to go without.

You might have a limit to how many each child can collect, and when they have their quota, direct them to another fun activity. You might want to enhance this by explaining that different colors have different point values, but not telling them what they are ahead of time! Points are totaled after they complete their collection. The person with the highest number of points might be given a silly prize such as a paper crown or hat.

Duck, Duck, Goose (#64)

Children sit in a circle. One player walks around the outside of the circle touching each seated player lightly on the head, saying "duck," "duck" while he does so. When he switches and says "goose," the one touched gets up and runs in the opposite direction to which the person who was "it" was walking. The object is to get back to that spot. The one who does not make it first is then "it."

Animal Blind Man's Bluff (#65)

The players form a circle around the "blind man" who stands blindfolded. He holds a long stick in his hand. When the leader says "Go!" the players move around the blind man, keeping their own places in the circle. He stops them by tapping his stick sharply on the ground. He then stretches his stick out in front of him. The player nearest to it takes hold of the end. The blind man then says, "Make a noise like a dog" or frog, pig, cat, or any other animal he may name. The player disguises his voice and makes the noise asked for. Should the blind man guess who the player is or should the player laugh, he changes places with the blind man.

The Farmer in the Dell (#66)

One child is selected as the farmer. He stands in the center of a circle made by other players. As they sing the words to this game they all march around the circle with hands joined. When they come to the words, "the farmer takes a wife," the player in the center chooses one of the circle players and leads her into the center of the circle with him. The sequence continues in this fashion using the sequence listed below, until the "cheese" is selected.

On the last verse all the circle players come into the circle and with those already in the center they all clap their hands over the head of the "cheese" while they sing the last verse. If the game is repeated, then the "cheese" becomes the farmer.

1. "The farmer in the dell, The farmer in the dell, Heigh-ho the derry oh, The farmer in the dell."

2. The farmer takes a wife
3. The wife takes a child
4. The child takes a nurse
5. The nurse takes a dog
6. The dog takes a cat
7. The cat takes a rat
8. The rat takes a cheese
9. The cheese stands alone

Blind Penny Hunt (#67)

Scatter pennies all over a field or floor. Blindfold all contestants with paper bags which they pull down over their faces (*do not use plastic bags*). Line them all up on a starting line. The leader says "Go!" The players look for pennies but the bag limits their vision to straight down. Players keep all the pennies they find. Players with the most and the fewest get prizes. Peanuts or wrapped candies may be used instead of pennies.

Variations: Play as above, but scatter a few nickels, dimes, and one silver dollar. There would be no need of prizes. Money found is the prize. Make sure there are no losers. Instead of money, small treasures may be scattered: wrapped suckers, balloons, pencils, small plastic toys, peanuts in the shell, small boxes of crayons.

Musical Animals (#68) *(a variation of musical chairs)*

Prepare ahead of time a number of animals cut out from magazines. Tell the children they will have to imitate these animals and give them suggestions for doing so. For example, hopping like a bunny, barking like a dog, interlocking thumbs to make hands like a butterfly fluttering, clasping hands and leaning over to let them hang down like an elephant's trunk, clasp hands over head for the long neck of a giraffe, etc. Have taped music. Scatter pictures face-up over the playing area. When the music starts, children move around. When the music stops, they stop and must imitate the animal to which they are nearest.

London Bridge (#69)

Two of the players face each other and form an archway by joining hands with their arms stretched upwards. The other players form a large circle and, as they sing, pass one at a time under the arch. The phrase, "My fair lady-O" in the second verse is the signal for the arch to fall and enclose the player who happens to be passing under at the time. This player is taken "off to prison" as the words indicate. This means that the two who form the arch take her away from the others then ask her which she would rather have: all the gold in the world, or all the silver in the world. When she has decided (her answer must be spoken quietly so the others don't hear), the arch is formed again and the "fair lady" stands directly behind the arch player who represents the choice she has made. The other children must not know which one represents gold and which silver.

When all the players have been caught and are lined up behind the two archway players, a tug-of-war between the "Gold" and "Silver" players ends the game. Don't forget a stout piece of rope.

"London bridge is falling down, falling down, falling down, London bridge is falling down, my fair Lady-O!"

"Build it up with sticks and stones, sticks and stones, sticks and stones, build it up with sticks and stones, my fair Lady-O!"

"Off to prison you must go, (etc)"

Chapter 3

GAMES for AGES 6-13

While there is a fairly large age spread here, children of these ages can usually quite successfully play group games together, which may be necessary depending on the size of your gathering. If there are many children, divide and choose appropriate games for each age group. Play characteristics become progressively more sophisticated, but children of all ages have great activity and energy in common. They all like chasing, hunting, and throwing games and slowly increase their personal skills and the ability to work in teams. See Chapter 5 for rambunctious outdoor games.

Here are a few rules to keep in mind when directing games for ages 6–13:

1. *Vary activities.* Even though everyone may be enjoying a game, don't let it go on too long. It's better to stop and move on to another game while the first one is at it's height, than waiting until interest wanes.

2. Keep control of the leadership. Explain, demonstrate if necessary, ask for questions. *When you have stated the rules, stick with them.* Children are notorious for wanting to change the rules to be to their advantage. Kindly explain that there are various ways to play some games, but you are going to play it as described this time, perhaps another time it could be played differently.

3. *Don't allow sides to be chosen.* This invariably leads to favoritism, or leaving out someone who may seem to be a disadvantage to a team. Rather, line children up from tallest to smallest, and count off into as many teams as may be needed—one, two, one, two, etc. For three teams, count to three; for four teams, count to four, etc.

4. To get two circles quickly, have all stand in one big circle. Then break the circle in half, with each half becoming a circle of its own. If an inner and outer circle is needed, designate which circle is which. Either of the above methods may also be used to choose relay teams.

5. To distinguish teams, have teams color-coded with ribbons, arm bands, or small squares of colored construction paper pinned to shirts.

6. If you are planning a number of games, vary between active games and quieter games. Plan for more games than you think you need. Better to have too many than too few! If a game doesn't catch on in the first few minutes, abandon it and go on to something else. Don't labor it.

7. It is often wise to have two game leaders, alternating the directing of the games. In that way, if there are props to prepare, one can be getting a game ready while the other is directing a game. They then switch roles.

CHILDREN'S MIXERS

Comic Book Characters (#70)

Put comic characters' names on pieces of paper, for example "Garfield," "Dennis the Menace," "Charlie Brown," "Superman," etc. Without allowing them to see who they represent, pin one name on each child's back. To learn their identity, they ask questions of other players. They can only ask questions that can be answered "yes" or "no" such as, "Am I an animal?" "Do I fly through the air?" Continue until most have guessed correctly.

Get Acquainted Yarn Pass (#71)

The children stand in a large circle. The leader passes the first child a ball of yarn. He takes the yarn then says his name (first name is enough if there are some younger children included) and where he lives. With his right hand he passes the yard around his left wrist on to the next child who repeats the procedure (without breaking the yarn, of course) and so on all around the circle until all are joined. The leader might say a *few* words about family ties. Then she instructs the last person who received the yarn to reverse the procedure. As the yarn is wound back up, each child tries to remember the name of the person who passed him the yarn, and where he came from.

Poor Kitty (#72) (ages 4–9)

Children sit on the floor or on chairs, in no particular formation, pretending they are cats. One player who is "it" strokes a kitty's head, while saying in a doleful tone, "poor kitty." The object is to make the kitty laugh but "it" cannot laugh in trying to do so. "It" may crawl on hands and knees and perform cat-like antics or meow pitifully. It may meow three times at each player to whom it pays a visit and if not successful in making the person laugh, must carry on to another. Some players pretend to lick a paw, watch a mouse hole or scratch themselves. If "it" succeeds in making a kitty laugh, that kitty then becomes "it." If "it" laughs, another person is assigned to be "it." You may have several kitties circulating at one time.

In and Out the Windows (#73)

The players form a circle by joining hands. One player who is "it" stands inside the circle. When the song begins, she skips around weaving in and out the circle under the joined hands of the players. When the players sing "Stand and face your partner," she stands in front of the person she happens to be nearest. She shakes hands with this person and, as the song indicates, "takes him off to London" by hooking her arm in his and skipping around the outside of the circle with him, while the circle closes ranks and skips in the opposite direction. For the next round the partner is the new "it" while the first "it" takes her place in the circle.

Go in and out the windows, (repeat three times)
As you have done before.

Now stand and face your partner, (repeat three times)
As you have done before.

Now take her off to London, (repeat three times)
As you have done before.

Midnight (#74)

Diagonally opposite corners of the ground or floor are marked off. In one is the Old Witch; in the other are the remaining players. A "safe" zone is clearly designated. The Old Witch goes forth and wanders about, being witchlike. The other players venture as near as they dare to the Witch, asking "What time is it, Old Witch?" If she answers "five o'clock," "nine o'clock," etc, they are safe. But when she says "Midnight!" they must run for home, the Old Witch chasing. The

Witch must not chase anyone until after she says "Midnight!" Anyone caught exchanges places with the Old Witch. When there are many players, there could be several Witches.

Cat and Mouse (#75)

The leader arranges couples facing each other (couples do not need to be boy/girl). Each couple should be about 12 feet from any other couples and spread out in an uneven pattern. One player is chosen to be the Cat and another the Mouse. Each couple now joins hands to form shelters for the Mouse. When the leader shouts "Go!" the Cat chases the Mouse. The Mouse dodges about and to escape being caught, it can slip into any one of the shelters before the Cat can get it. The couples forming the shelters hold their arms as far apart as possible to help the Mouse, but they must keep their hands joined and must not move from their places. The Mouse is momentarily safe until the leader again shouts "Go!" when the Mouse must abandon its present shelter and head for another one. When the Mouse is caught, it becomes the Cat, and the Cat becomes the Mouse, and the game continues. When both have been caught, a new Cat and Mouse are chosen. If there is quite a large group, you might choose several Cats and Mice, but each Cat must catch her designated Mouse.

Snow Removal Race (#76)

In spite of its title, this is an all season race. Divide into teams. Have a strip of plastic on the ground for each team. On this plastic scatter popped corn, which represents the "snow." Try to have an equal amount of snow for each team. Players spread out along their designated piece of plastic, down on their knees. They may prop themselves on their elbows if necessary but may not use their hands. At the word "Go!" they all lean down and clear the plastic by eating the popcorn. Leader should emphasize "no hands!" First team to clear their snow wins. This can also be played with individual participants instead of teams.

Locomotive (#77)

Form a large circle and then break it up into 3's. The three people in each group stand one behind the other with hands on the waist of the one in front. These are the locomotives and they all face what was the center of the circle. One person is chosen to be the caboose. The caboose tries to hook on to the end of any of the locomotives. The locomotives try to prevent him from hooking on by swinging from side to side or by turning clear around if necessary, but they must not let go of each other's waists. If the caboose succeeds in hooking on, the one in front of the locomotive must leave and become the caboose.

LOCOMOTIVES

CABOOSE

Bean Bag (#78)

Players stand in a circle. The leader selects one of the players as "it" and gives a bean bag to one of the others. At a given signal, the bean bag is thrown quickly from one person to another, trying to keep it away from "it." If "it" catches the bag, she exchanges places in the circle with the last person touching the bag. If "it" touches the person holding the bag, they also exchange places. To be effective, the bag should be thrown as soon as it is received.

Crows and Cranes (#79)

Divide players into teams: one called crows and the other cranes. Both teams line up across the play area facing each other about six feet apart. A safety zone is drawn or designated about 30' behind each line of players. The leader stands in midfield to the side and shouts either crows or cranes. If the leader calls crows, the crows run and are chased by the cranes. If a crow is tagged by a crane before she reaches safety behind an appointed goal line, she becomes a crane. Both groups line up quickly again after each series and the leader again shouts either crows or cranes. The leader should make her call as unpredictable as possible to heighten suspense. The team with the most players when time is called is the winner.

Flying Dutchman (#80)

The players form a large circle and clasp each others' hands. Two players are selected to be the "Flying Dutchmen." These two run around the outside of the circle holding hands. Suddenly the inside

player of the two tags the clasped hands of two of the circle players. These two immediately run in the opposite direction of the "Flying Dutchmen." Thus the game becomes a race between the couples to be the first around the circle. The first couple back to the starting place fills in the vacant spot while the other couple is the "Flying Dutchmen" for the next round.

Nations (#81)

Players are arranged in several small groups of equal size, each bearing the name of a nation and each nation having a circle drawn for its homebase (flour can be used to draw a circle or just use an old shirt to designate homebase). The leader throws a ball against the side of a building or tree, or if there is nothing against which to throw, she may toss it up. As it bounces back or comes down, she calls the name of a nation. The players of that nation rush for the ball and then run for their homebase trying not to be caught by the other players. Those caught join the nation by whom they were caught. The game is up when one nation has caught all the others. "Caught" can mean either "tagged" or "restrained," depending on how rough you want the game to be. Team members may or may not be allowed to protect their teammate with the ball by blocking the others, again depending on how rough the game is to be.

Knee Walk (#82)

Each participant sits back on heels and grasps insteps with hands. In this position he tilts forward to his knees, keeping feet off the floor and hitches forward on his knees, using first one knee, then the other. Object: to walk on knees 10 feet without losing balance or grip on insteps.

Statues (#83)

One player who is "it" hides his eyes against a tree, wall or fence while all the others line up at a starting line some thirty or more feet away. When all are ready, "it" calls "Go!" and counts to ten out loud. While he counts, all the other players are moving as rapidly as possible toward the goal where he stands. On "ten" he turns around. Every player must then "freeze" so that "it" does not catch him moving. If "it" catches anyone moving, the culprit must return to the starting line. "It" then turns around and counts to ten again. The players then resume their journey toward the goal line. This process is repeated until one of the players reaches the goal line. This player then becomes "it" for the next round. A variation is for each player to announce what statue she will represent during the game. Then, if a person is caught moving *or* does not freeze in the attitude of her designated statue, she must return to the starting line.

Fox and Geese (#84)

The outline of a large wheel with spokes is marked on the ground with a white powder (flour works well) or in winter the wheel can be tramped in the snow. A person designated as the fox stands in the center of the wheel. The other players (the geese) try to escape the fox as he chases them along the spokes or circumference of the wheel. When tagged, a goose becomes the fox. This may also be played in damp sand on a beach where it's easier to see if a person veers off the spokes or circumference of the wheel.

Three Deep (#85)

Players stand in a double circle with one player standing directly behind every player in the inner circle (they're facing in). The "Chaser" is on the inside of the circles and "It" stands outside. The

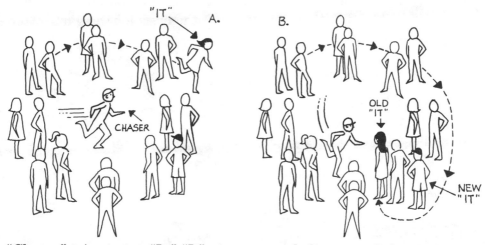

"Chaser" tries to tag "It." "It" may run or dodge around the circle as long as he wants, but if tagged, "Chaser" and "It" change places. "It" may get someone else to be "It" by managing to get into the circle without being tagged and standing in front of any players who are standing two deep. If this happens, the person who is on the outside of the circle becomes "It." Action continues with the new "It" until "Chaser" succeeds in tagging him or he manages to stand three deep.

North, South, East, West (#86)

Newspapers or pieces of cardboard are spread around in six different places at least 25' apart. Each place is designated as a specific state or province (e.g. New York, California, Florida, Ohio, B.C., Ontario, etc.). Each state is given a designated population so that only that number of people are allowed there at any one time. This population should be written on the newspapers or cardboard with a heavy marking pen. The players distribute themselves among the states, not exceeding the populations, and one person is "it." At a given signal, "it" calls the names of two states. Those states called must then exchange two individuals.

"It" tries to tag those who pass from one state to another. The first one tagged becomes "it" and the game continues. When a state is called that is not designated, then everyone must leave their state and find another, but there must still be only the correct population at each state. If one state has too many people, the last to arrive must try to find another state. This may also be played using different countries instead of states. If you have a number of national origins in your family tree, use those countries as the basis for the game. Stop playing before enthusiasm wanes.

Bubble Gum Race (#87)

Give each player a piece of bubble gum. The first person to blow a bubble at least 3" in diameter wins a prize. Also, the last person to blow a bubble wins another piece of bubble gum because he needs help.

TAG GAMES

Of all games, tag is probably the most common and rarily requires any equipment. In cases where some equipment is needed, see that this is on hand. Usually no special area is required and it can be played by any number from two to over fifty. One player is "it" and chases other players until he tags one. The tagged one now becomes "it." In most games of tag, some base is decided upon which makes a player "safe" while touching it. Here are a few variations of tag:

Chinese Tag (#88)

The tagged player is "it" and must hold the part of the body where he was tagged.

Swat Tag (#89)

"It" tags others with a swatter (rolled up newspaper, etc.) then drops it. The new "it" must pick up the swatter and continue.

Cross Tag (#90)

One player ("it") chases another. Some other player may run in between "it" and the one being chased. This crossing goes on indefinitely and "it" must always chase the last person who ran between him and the one he was chasing. Anyone who is tagged becomes "it."

Link Tag (#91)

Designate a base. Two players link hands and try to tag the other players. These two players are the only ones who can tag others throughout the game. All those tagged take their places between the first two players, all linking hands. The chain grows longer with each new addition. The players being chased may try to break the chain by forcing clasped hands apart while avoiding the two players at either end of the chain. If the chain is broken, it must be joined again before the tagging can continue. Players dropping out to rest must return to base and remain there until they re-enter the game. Players may not return to base to escape being tagged.

Shadow Tag (#92)

Requires a sunny day. To tag a person, "it" must step on that person's shadow.

Chain Tag (#93)

This is a variation of link tag. The players are scattered around a designated area with boundaries. Two captains are chosen. At the starting signal, the two captains try to tag as many players as possible. The first person tagged links hands with the captain, and they run together. As each person is tagged, he joins the line. The line may encircle a player, but only the captain may tag him. The longest line wins and the last player to escape being tagged wins. If the lines are fairly even, they may be used to form lines for another game.

Flashlight Tag (#94)

This game must be played in deep shade or darkness. "It" has only to zap a wanderer in the dark with a beam of light from his flashlight to tag him and thus convert the wanderer into "it." Those being chased must keep on the move to avoid being zapped. This game is most popular in late summer when the sun sets a little earlier but the nights are still warm. It's best to set boundaries and provide adult supervision to keep younger children from getting "lost" or scared. Check the terrain out in daylight to make sure there are no holes, water or other dangers.

Color Tag (#95)

Played the same as plain tag but there are colored squares scattered around—colored paper will do. Players are safe when standing on a colored square but a player may stand on each color only once. For example, if he takes refuge from "it" on a red square, he must not use a red square again, but must next run to another color.

Ball Tag (#96)

Use a nerf ball (soft foam) or a bean bag. "It" has the ball which he throws at any other player. The other player may attempt to dodge. If he is hit, he becomes "it."

RELAYS

There are literally hundreds of ways to run relays. We'll include just a few. You'll be able to dream up lots more on your own. Also see the cross-reference section under "Relays."

Tunnel Relay (#97)

Buy a 20 foot strip of plastic or durable material and make a tunnel out of it by stapling or sewing the sides together. Plastic may be purchased in large rolls at building supply stores, hardware stores, or garden centers. Some large toy stores may have plastic tubes readymade. The tunnel should be about three feet in diameter.

Select two teams. Each team puts half of its members at either end of the tube. Two opponents start crawling through the tunnel from opposite ends and must inevitably pass each other in the middle. When passing, they should not interfere with each other. When they reach the other end, they tag a teammate who starts back through. The first team finished wins but the most fun is watching the wiggling tunnel from the outside.

Zig-Zag Relay (#98)

Players are divided into two or more equal teams, each of which is divided into two ranks. The two divisions of each team stand about 8 feet apart and facing each other. At the command "Go!" the first person in the first rank throws a ball to the first person in the opposite rank. This player quickly throws it to the second player in the first rank, and so on, zig-zagging to the end of the line, where the ball is immediately returned by the same way. The group getting the ball back to the start first wins.

IST TEAM   2ND TEAM

Flag Relay (#99) (use scarves or kerchiefs for flags)

(See illustration, next page.) Each team of 4–8 players should have a flag of a different color. Half of a team stands directly opposite the other half, which is 30 feet distant. The runners stand in file formation, one directly behind the other. There should be a space of 4–5 feet between each file. The first runner for each team is given a flag, one flag to a team. All players start from one side, as in the diagram. On the word "Go!" the players with the flags race to the players opposite and hand the flag to the first runner in line. This second runner must not step forward to take the flag. When a player hands over the flag he should go immediately to the end of the line to avoid interfering with the next player. The second runner races to the next player, etc, until every runner has carried their team's flag. The running distance may vary, depending on the age of the runners and the size of the available playing area.

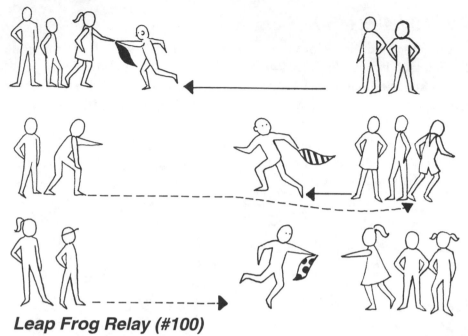

Leap Frog Relay (#100)

Players stand about 8 feet apart, one behind the other. All players in a column, except the last player, assume a squatting/stooping position, hands on knees. At a signal, the last player leap frogs over the backs of the players in front of him and then assumes a stooping position about 8 feet in front of the last person he leaped over. The last person left in the line then continues in this manner and when the player who originally headed the column reaches the front of the column again, he runs forward and crosses an indicated goal line, thus finishing the race. In other words, everyone on a team leapfrogs once, then the front person runs toward a goal line. The goal line must be judiciously placed so that the runner runs about 50 feet.

Over-and-Under Leap Frog Relay (#101)

The players form up in lines (minimum of four per line), odd numbers standing with feet astride and even numbers making a "back" for leap frog. The last player in each column stands behind a line and at the signal crawls between the legs of those standing astride, and leaps over the backs of the others. That player makes his way to the front of the team in this manner, and then assumes the appropriate stance, which is the opposite stance of the person behind him. The person who is left last in line then proceeds forward in the same manner. If space is limited, the whole team can move back as each new player gets to the head of the line. The relay is finished when they are all back in their original positions in line. First team to finish wins. *Variations:* go through the rotation more than once or go for distance.

Chariot Relay (#102)

This is the same as any running relay, except that two, three or four players hook arms and run together. They round a given point and on returning to their line they touch off the next members of their team. This may be made very interesting and spectacular if some of the players, acting as horses, pull a driver around on a piece of cardboard or tarp or other suitable substitute for a chariot.

Skin the Snake (#103)

Sometimes called Chinese Relay. Teams of five to ten players line up in single file. Each player stoops over, puts his right hand between his legs, and grasps the left hand of the player behind him. At the signal "Go!" the last person in line lies down on her back, putting her feet between the legs of the player in front of her. The line walks back-

ward, straddling the bodies of the other members of the team, each player lying down in turn. As soon as all are flat on their backs, the *last* person gets up and starts back, pulling up the next person after her, and so on, until the players are all in their original starting positions. Players must not let go of hands. A partial demonstration is important to see that they all get the idea. It's a good game to repeat, to see if they can decrease their time from start to finish. This game is also loads of fun to do without the competitive factor. All ages can participate and have a great time with no goal other than fun.

Skin the Snake Race (#104)

Same formation as the last game: players reach back between their legs with their right hands and grasp the left hand of the player behind. The entire column assumes this starting position. However, at the signal, the whole column shuffle-runs around a designated goal, and returns to the starting line. The first team back wins, provided the column has not been broken.

Skin the Snake Biathalon (#105)

To make this a "biathalon event," combine the above two races, completing the shuffle, then continuing with "skin the snake" feature as the second stage. All must be performed without losing their grasp.

Caterpillar (#106)

Get everyone lying down on their stomachs side by side, packed really close together. The person at the end of the line rolls over onto her neighbor and keeps rolling down the road of bodies. When she gets to the end she lays on her stomach and the next person proceeds down the road. First team finished wins.

Worm Relay (#107) (4–8 players per team)

Players sit on the ground in a straight line and place their feet in the lap and hands on the waist of the player in front of them. Only the player in the front on the line may allow her feet to touch the ground. The finish line is only ten feet away but the entire worm must cross the line.

SOME FAVORITE ACTIVE GAMES
(for "Rambunctious Games," see Chapter 5)

Kick the Can (#108)

The player selected as "it" places a can on a base position and stands over the can, eyes closed, while counting to 100. The players hide and "it" goes looking for them when she finishes counting. If "it" sees a player in hiding, she calls that player's name. That player is then caught and must return to base. "It" continues to look for hiding players, but must also keep a close watch on the can because if any player sneaks from his hiding place and kicks the can, the hiding players may change hiding positions, and the players already caught by "it" may hide again. When the can is kicked off base, all players are safe and remain so until "it" has replaced the can on base, then "it" goes seeking the hiding players again. After all the players have been caught, the player who was caught first becomes "it" for the next game.

Run, Sheep, Run (#109)

Two equal sides are chosen, each with a captain. One group is the sheep, the other the hunters. Home base is chosen. The hunters close their eyes and the sheep go and hide all together. The sheep leader comes back when they are hidden and goes along with the hunters as they hunt for the sheep. When the sheep leader thinks an opportune time has came, he yells "Run, sheep, run!" All the sheep immediately rush for home base as do the hunters. If the first sheep beats the first hunter to home base, they switch sides. If not, the sheep hide again. The sheep captain may choose pre-arranged signals to shout while the hunters are hunting, e.g. "armadillo" = danger; "jack rabbit" = get ready to run; "cucumber" = coming closer; etc.

Sardines (#110)

One player hides while the rest close their eyes and count to 100. When the counting is finished, they all set out to find the player who hid. Whenever anyone finds the hider, she doesn't let on, but waits for a chance when she thinks no one is looking to join him. Hiders soon are packed in. When the last finder discovers the spot, the game starts over, the first finder becoming the hider.

Steal the Bacon (#111)

Sides are chosen, players evenly divided, and lined up as follows:

1	2	3	4	5	6	7	8	9	10	11	12
				Bacon							
12	11	10	9	8	7	6	5	4	3	2	1

The two sides stand about 20 feet apart, the bacon in the middle. Any object can be the bacon such as a block of wood or rolled up newspaper. The leader calls numbers and decides points in disputes.

When the game starts, the leader calls a number, e.g. "two," where upon #2 from each side makes a run for the bacon. The person who secures the bacon makes a point for her side. The game should continue at least until each person has had a chance to steal the bacon.

Tiger Trap (#112)

The players are divided into two teams of equal size. One team, the Tiger Trap, holds hands in a line and starts at one end of the play area, which should be about 80' square. The others, the Tigers, spread out over the entire play area but must not go outside it. When the leader calls "Go!" the players forming the Trap run after the Tigers. They try to catch the Tigers by encircling them. The Tigers try to escape around the closing ends of the Trap or by ducking under the arms of the Trap players. Those caught are out of the game and stand just outside the play area. The game continues until all the Tigers are caught, or the players may change over after five minutes of play. *Variation:* Allow no ducking under the arms of the Trap players.

Hidden People (#113)

Divide into 2 or more groups (3 or 4 groups is best). Each group picks a person to hide and makes this person known to the other teams. Each team may communicate with their hidden person in any way before she leaves, so that they know where she will be. At the signal, the "hidden people" hide within specified boundaries. All other players must remain in a group for five minutes. At the next signal, the search for all opposing "hidden people" begins. When found, each must return to home base without struggle. The team of the last hidden person to be brought back is the winner.

Treasure Hunt (#114)

1. This can be planned around a specific theme. For example, a pirate hunt (eye patches, cardboard knives, sea chant); a storybook with each person a different character; a nature hunt; an Indian hunt using Indian signs for clues.

2. Use clues everyone will understand.

3. Lay the trail *backwards*—decide where the treasure will be hidden, hide it, then write clues.

4. Don't hide the treasure too near the starting place.

5. Put the hardest clue in the middle of the hunt, allowing stragglers to catch up.

6. Read the first clue to everyone out loud to get everyone off to the same start.

G-Man (#115)
(7–10 players, may have several games going at once.)

The leader selects a G-Man who turns his back and covers his eyes while players are lined up behind him. When the leader says, "Look," the G-Man is given one minute to look at the players, after which he turns around again and covers his eyes. The leader then motions one player to leave the line and keep out of sight. The line is then rearranged, and the G-Man turns around and is asked to name or describe the missing player. Whether the G-Man has succeeded or failed, the player who left the line becomes the G-Man for the next game.

Chapter 4

SPECIAL GAMES for TEENS

Teens will enjoy many of the games listed in other sections of this book, such as "Couple Balloon Stunt," "Swat," "Balloon Stomp," "Lifesaver Relay," "Spoon on a String," and almost all the "rambunctious" games in Chapter 5, but here are a few more that are especially for them.

If your gathering is more than one day long, feature a special activity for teens to get to know and have fun with cousins their own age: a chaperoned trip to a special location, a wave pool or giant slide, a shopping trip, bowling, roller-skating. Something all their own. If a committee plans your gatherings, consider having a teen or two on the committee. There is no better way to get the teens interested.

Sir Walter Raleigh (#116)

Contestants: 2 couples, boy/girl. Equipment: 2 rags (2' x 2') for each pair.

Remember the tale, true or not, of Sir Walter Raleigh gallantly laying down his cloak so Queen Elizabeth would not have to step in water? This game is a take-off on his chivalry. Choose 2 "Sir Walter's," and 2 "Queen Elizabeth's." Outline a circular or oval course about 20–30 feet in diameter, either around a row of chairs, a group of spectators or some other obstacle that will separate the couples. Place one couple at either end of the course. Give each boy two rags which serve as "cloaks" in the contest. Upon the word "go" the boy lays down one rag, the girl steps on it. He then lays down the second as rapidly as possible, whips the first around for his "Queen" to step on, and so on around the course. The object is to be able to catch up with and tag the other couple, both moving in the same direction. The couple that gets the rhythm flowing smoothly will be the winners. The contest ends when one couple manages to catch up with and tag the opposing couple. This is as much fun for the spectators as the players.

Squirt (#117)

Equipment: An inexpensive plastic raincoat, a water pistol and a candle for each contestant.

This is another contest in which the spectators enjoy observing the shenanigans of the contestants. It can be done by one couple but it is more fun to watch several sets of contestants at once. It also turns into a contest to see which couple can hold out the longest.

Choose the contestants *before* telling them what the stunt will be, a boy and a girl for each team. Each pair will stand facing each other at a distance of about four feet apart. Dress each one in a raincoat. Give each a filled water pistol which they may not "shoot" until the word "go." Then give each a lighted candle. (Obviously, the contestants must be mature and responsible enough to be able to keep the candles away from the plastic raincoats.) The object of the game is to be able to put out your opponent's candle while protecting your own. No hiding candles under clothing or raincoats. Of course, some will be more concerned with getting their opponent soaked rather than putting out the candle but that's all part of the fun! Winner is the person who manages to keep his/her candle lit the longest.

Tangle (#118)

Choose one person to leave the room or area. Have all the rest stand in a large circle, firmly clasping hands. Without letting go, they must weave themselves in and out to make a large "tangle." They may do anything they like to get themselves into a knot but *may not let go of hands*. People will find themselves in hilarious positions. When they are in a great mess, the person sent out comes in and tries to "untie the knot," again without the people in the tangle letting go hands. It will be easier for the person who is trying to untangle the knot if he can stand on a chair or stool to better see what he needs to do. Sometimes it takes a while before he accomplishes his task—there are occasions when he will make it worse rather than better!

Double Decker Tug-of-War (#119)

You need two equal teams. This may be done with just boys participating or with boys as the "horses" and girls as the "riders." Players team up with as many "horse/rider" combinations as possible. Line up in regular tug-of-war formation, however only the "riders" are permitted to touch the rope.

The contest is conducted in the usual tug-of-war manner, each team attempting to pull the other over a designated line. Any rider who falls off her horse or touches the ground while still holding the rope puts herself and her horse out of the competition. However, if the rider lets go of the rope *before* falling off the horse, they may return to the competition when mounted again. The game is won when one team is able to pull the other over the line or touch the wall behind them with the end of their rope (if it's held in a gym).

One Minute Walk (#120)

If you have had a number of lively games, you may want to use this quiet one. Map out a course up to 80 feet long. Any number of contestants may be involved in this game. Line up the players along a starting line. The object is that they must cover the course in exactly one or two minutes, or whatever length of time you have predetermined. Confiscate all wrist watches and make sure there are no clocks on the wall (if indoors). Upon the word "go," they all set off over the course. They may go as slowly as they like but must keep moving forward. When all the players have finished, the time-keeper announces who finished closest to the allotted time. You might offer a prize for this one—how about a very inexpensive mickey-mouse watch?

Sardines in the Dark (#121)

This is best played either at night or in a totally dark room. One player is sent away to hide. The rest have to grope silently in the dark and try to find where he is hiding. Upon finding him, they hide with him. If this is in a small place, it can become hilarious as they all try to remain silent. Keep playing until the last person finds the person hiding.

Wink (#122)

Players are divided into two groups. One group is seated on chairs in a circle, the others stand behind the chairs. It works well with girls on the chairs and the boys standing behind them but if the group is not evenly divided between boys and girls, it doesn't really matter. One chair in the circle is left empty but there is a player behind it. The player with the empty chair tries to "steal" a girl from another chair by winking at her. If she sees the wink, she must try to escape to his chair. However, her partner standing behind her may stop her by touching her. (He needn't actually restrain her—a touch is enough). To make it more difficult, the boys must stand with their hands behind their backs until they see their girl trying to escape. The person left with the empty chair then tries to capture another girl. The game continues for 20 minutes or until interest flags.

Water Drop (#123)

Divide into teams of not more than 10 people each. The group lies in a circle facing the center with their legs in the air. The leader places a plastic dishpan of water on top of the player' feet. The object is for everyone to remove their shoes without spilling the water. To do this, one person at a time brings their legs down and removes their shoes. The others, meanwhile, are still holding up the pan of water. If the water is dropped, a new dishpan is placed on their feet and the game continues. The first team to get their shoes off wins.

Chapter 5

HIKING GAMES and RAMBUNCTIOUS GAMES

This chapter covers hikes (which can be anywhere from quite easy to quite strenuous), and *very* active outdoor games of the type that could be considered "rough-and-tumble" games. We call them *rambunctious* games. This latter type is enjoyed by older boys but some older girls are likely to join in, too. After all, these games are no rougher than soccer, which girls participate in quite commonly.

HIKING GAMES

If there is time and space, and you have qualified people who are willing to supervise these activities, hiking games (or just plain hikes) can be great for entertaining older children and young teens. Or a short, easy hike could include anyone of any age (with proper supervision). Obviously, no intelligent leader would take a group into woods or unknown territory without making proper plans. Here are a few basics to keep in mind when planning a hike:

Destination: You must know where and how far you are going, the time it will take and the travel conditions. Try to take a "dry run" by yourself beforehand to be able to estimate these conditions within reason. This will also teach you about topography, obstacles and interest points enroute. Always secure permission to cross private property.

Check the following:

1. The weather report for the 24 hours before setting out.

2. Know when dark comes in the geographical location you are in.

3. Always carry basic first aid supplies.

4. Explain to hikers about taking sensible clothing and footwear. "Layering" is a wise idea if you are in a cool climate: many light items that can be added or removed as needed. Shoes should be well worn-in. Other considerations are rain gear, insect repellent, sunblock, sunhat, flashlight and whistle (for a lost person to signal with). It may be wise to have basic clothing and equipment requirements for participation.

5. Food, water, cooking requirements (if any). Carry your own water supply or check for officially tested water. If your destination is a beach or a place where it is safe and permissible to have a campfire, a great meal is "Hobo Stew." See Chapter 9 for instructions for "Hobo Stew" and other fun food ideas.

Hobo Hike (#124)

Give each Hobo a "bandana handkerchief" (a large piece of calico or other brightly colored material) lined with aluminum foil and containing wieners, rolls, pickles, doughnuts, fruit and marshmallows. Each bundle is tied from opposite corners in knots so that it may be carried on a stick. Sticks are also provided.

If many of the young cousins do not know each other, have two of each type of cloth for bandanas. They have to find the matching one who is their partner. These two walk side by side and get acquainted.

You might prime them with suggestions before they start—for example, they can tell about hobbies, things they hate most, things they like most, etc. After about 10 minutes on the trail, the leader signals, and all persons on the right move up one, with the front person going to the back. Thus they have new partners to get acquainted with. Continue with partner changes every 10–15 minutes. After the tramp, a campfire is made (if permissible), perhaps some games are played, and they eat the food in their bandanas.

Adventure Hike (#125)

Start out in the morning, carrying supplies for lunch. Have a chosen destination. Divide into groups of about 8–10, each with a leader. Each group hikes to the destination by a different route. When they all get there, each group tells its story. Tales may be tall, but must be based on some fact, e.g. a chipmunk crossing the trail may be embroidered to be a "wild animal." After each group tells its tale, vote to determine the best tale. After the meal, play a game or two.

Hare and Hounds Hike (#126)

Divide the group into two—a small, quick group, and a larger group of all the rest. The "Hares" are given a destination, a five minute head start and a big bag of oatmeal, or something that will not leave litter or harm the environment. They lay a clear trail as they go, including obstacles, false trails that lead nowhere, and trails that go in circles. (One "Hare" may go off on a side trail, end it abruptly, and then cut across ground to rejoin the rest of the "Hares.") Hounds, however, may never take shortcuts. They must keep on the trails at all times, and backtrack if they follow a false clue. The "Hounds" follow the trails and try to catch the "Hares" before they get to their destination. At the goal, an assistant guide may be laying a fire and preparing for a marshmallow roast.

Mystery Hike (#127) (see "Mystery Walk," #141)

Write out a series of clues to be figured out. Each clue leads the group to a spot where the next clue is hidden. With a large group, divide into teams of three or four and start each team at a different point, or at different times. Explain that they *must* leave clues where they find them. Keep a master list of all clues and the places where they were hidden. The hike should end with some sort of surprise such as a treat, campfire, etc.

Sounds (#128)

While resting on a hike, or at any quiet time, ask each person to be very still and write down every sound they hear during five minutes. The lists will vary considerably, and it will be fun to see who has the sharpest ears. You may hear the rustle of leaves, chirping of a cricket, several bird sounds, a snapping twig, the breathing of the group, the wind and many other sounds. Take pencils and paper.

Number One Person (#129)

This game is best if the group does not exceed 15. The leader points to some plant or other object, turning to the first in line and asking its name or something about it. If the first person answers correctly, she retains her position. If not, she must go to the end of the line, and number two becomes Number One Person. The object is to remain Number One Person as long as possible.

Good Turn (#130)

Set aside 15 minutes on a hike perhaps after lunch, for a "Good Turn." Each hiker is to do a good turn in the woods in that time and report on it or show it to the group. Clearing the trail of dangerous stones, removing a fallen branch, picking up or burying trash or debris, all constitute "good turns." Watch the hikers lest in their zeal the good turn does more harm than good!

Quest (#131)

Make a list of probable "discoveries" which may be found on a hike. Give a copy to each hiker or team of from four to six people. For the beginners in the field of nature, the list may include such things as two kinds of spider webs, a bird's nest, or winged seeds. For more experienced people, the names of specific plants or animals may be given. Give each item a score value according to the difficulty in finding it; such as spider's web =1; bird's nest =5. The highest score at the end of the hike wins. When discovered, the objects are pointed out to everyone (but not removed), and only the discoverer gets the score. As a variation of this game, divide the group in half and ask one group to look for the listed objects on the right side of the trail, and the other on the left.

Spot Spy (#132)

This game is great fun when a group is resting on a hike or loitering along the way. The leader says, "I can see 5 white oaks." The group is given one or two minutes to spot the white oaks. All those who see them may indicate this by sitting down, taking off their hats, or by some other agreed upon signal. All those who see the object(s) receive a point.

RAMBUNCTIOUS GAMES (for ages 10 and up)

Ante Over (#133)

Two teams are on opposite sides of a building—the bigger, the better (no flat roofs). One player calls "ante over" and throws the ball (use a soft rubber ball or tennis ball). Everyone on the other team tries to catch it. If someone succeeds, he and all his teammates dart around the building with the ball and try to hit one of the opponents with the ball. Meanwhile, the other team is trying to escape around to the other side of the building. If the thrower succeeds in hitting someone with the ball, the hit player must join the thrower's side and the same team throws over the roof again. If he does not succeed in hitting anyone, he joins the other team and the ball is given to the other team. If no one catches the ball when it is thrown over the building, the side that failed to catch it calls "ante over" and throws it back. If the ball fails to go over the building or rolls back, the side throwing calls out "pig's tail." The side wins which gains all or most players.

Wells-Fargo (#134)

Materials: wide masking tape, 3 small boxes marked 25, 50, 75. A pretend fort is marked off, approximately 10'x10'.

The group is split into two teams, Soldiers and Bank Robbers (or Good Guys and Bad Guys). The boxes marked with numbers are gold bricks which are given to the Soldiers at the beginning. The Bank Robbers have the fort surrounded and the Soldiers are outside the fort trying to get the gold past the Bank Robbers and into the fort. The Bank Robbers try to capture the gold before it gets into the fort. When all the gold is in the fort or the Bank Robbers have captured it, the game is over. Each person has a piece of masking tape attached to the back of his hand or shirt, which represents his "life." A person is "killed" by pulling the tape off and keeping it for points. The teams should be marked in some way to tell them apart—perhaps with colored tape. Each "life" (tape) is worth one point. Once a person is "killed" he is out of the game but he keeps his captured tapes for counting later. The team with the most points (tapes + gold) wins. Gold is captured by pulling the tape off the person who has possession of it.

Capture the Flag (#135)

Territory: Divide in half as evenly as possible. The division line and outer boundaries should be clearly explained to all players. The size should be determined by terrain, time of day and amount of playing time. Usually the size should be a football field or larger.

Flags: Each side has a distinctive flag on a movable pole at least 8 feet high and perpendicular to the ground.

Arm Bands: Every player wears an arm band (single band of 1" gauze) tied somewhere between the wrist and shoulder. One side ties it on the left arm, the other the right. These bands must not be covered with any clothing, nor changed from one arm to the other.

Game: When all bands have been given out, each team takes its flag and places it somewhere within its own territory. After ten minutes a whistle or bugle blows and the game starts. The first team to bring the opponents' flag to the game leader wins the game. Some from each team try to capture the opponents' flag; others try to defend their flag. A person is "killed" by having his arm band torn off. A person may play only when he has his arm band on. When it is torn off, he must go back to the leader and obtain a new band.

Special Rules:

1. In fighting, there must be no dirty play (e.g. slugging, kicking).

2. The flag may be moved during the game.

3. No one may use an arm band taken from another person. He must get a new one.

4. No one is allowed in or under any building or shelter or in any tree.

5. Anyone going out of bounds must forfeit his arm band.

6. Announce the game's end by a loud blast on a whistle or bugle.

Organ Donors (#136) *(a take-off on Capture the Flag)*

Players are divided into two teams. Each team has various organs represented by individual players. For example, heart, brain, liver, kidneys, arms, legs, etc. There can be many minor organs such as toes, fingers, hair, nose, etc, as are needed to allow everyone to represent an organ. Each team also has a Captain who does not represent an organ and whose job is to reassign organs, as needed.

All players receive 3x5 cards tied around their wrists naming their organs. Each team has a different colored card. Players must keep these cards in plain view and not hold on to them. The teams have a minute or so to spread out and hide anywhere on the playing field. Then a whistle is blown, signaling the start of the game.

Players try to rip off opponent's cards while keeping their own intact. If a player rips off a card, he takes it to the Clinic where he receives points for his team. For instance, a heart may be worth 2000 points, a brain 1500 points, and other organs worth 500–1000 points each, depending on the organ. These points are all figured out ahead of time and posted. A player can bring in only one card at a time. If a person's tag is ripped off, she must go get a new card tied on by the Clinic and take it to her Captain to receive a new organ assignment. The Captain keeps a list of organs of her team so that new organ assignments are made in the order of importance to the body. For example, hearts, brains, kidneys, and livers must be assigned before other organs. A person's organ can change each time it is ripped off. After a certain time, a whistle is blown signaling the end of the game. The team with the most points wins. Or the first team to reach (say) 20,000 points wins.

Note: The Clinic can be anywhere on or off the field, is the only safe zone, and should be manned by at least 3 people. The Captains may remain in one place or roam around. The game is best played in an area with many trees and good places to hide and sneak up on people. The general rules of Capture the Flag (above) apply.

[Adapted by Norm Derkson, Youth Pastor, Foothills Alliance Church, Calgary, AB.]

COMBATIVE GAMES

The following are combative games, performed by two people. The winner of each round is usually challenged by someone else and an overall champion is determined by this elimination process.

Rooster Fight (#137)

Draw a circle on the ground. Two participants squat within the circle, each placing a stick under their knees with arms under the stick, hands clasped in front of their knees. At a signal, each tries to tip the opponent over or out of the circle.

Indian Leg Wrestle (#138)

Participants lie on their backs, side by side, legs extended in opposite directions, belts even. Adjoining legs are raised vertically and lowered three times to the leader counting "one, two, three." At "three," legs are locked together at the knees and each tries to bring the opponent's leg down to the floor, which turns the loser on his face.

Indian Arm Wrestle (#139)

Clasp right hands, brace right feet against each other, outer edges touching. Left foot should be well to the rear to give firm support. In this position each tries to make the other move either of his feet, or to touch the ground with any part of the body other than the feet. It's harder to do on a log. *Variation:* The back foot can be moved.

Travois Race, #155

Chapter 6   CROSS-GENERATIONAL GAMES
(Co-operative and Noncompetitive)
ETHNIC GAMES, BUILDING PROJECTS

Co-operative and noncompetitive games are really the best types of games for family gatherings. With most of these games, no one wins but no one loses either. And the best part is that the movements in these games are often slower which allows for a wider range of participants (young, old, handicapped). Such games we call cross-generational games because almost any age can play.

Streets and Alleys (#140) *(minimum 12–16 players)*

This is a co-operative game where most participants are relatively inactive and two people (or perhaps four or six) are *very* active. Make sure appropriate people are chosen to be active. It's also great fun to watch.

Line players up facing in one direction in straight rank and file, like a marching band. Try to square up the group so that there are close to the same number of people in each direction. For example, if you have 30 participants, line them up in 6 rows of 5 people in each row. Space them approximately 6 feet apart.

The Leader stands in front of the group, facing them. The players stretch out their arms, approximately touching the hands of the people on either side of them. This makes a series of "streets." There is a Runner, a Chaser, and a Leader. When the Leader blows a whistle or shouts "streets," the Chaser chases the Runner down the "streets" and tries to tag him. At the next whistle or when the Leader shouts "alleys," all those with arms out-stretched make a quarter turn to the right. This makes a new set of "alleys." Neither Runner nor Chaser may duck under or pass through the out-stretched arms. Each time the Leader blows the whistle or shouts, there is a quarter turn to the right. The Leader who uses her whistle wisely will make this a very interesting game. When the Runner is tagged, another couple is chosen. If they are too well-matched, it may be necessary to change couples so the game does not become too long. If the group is very large, more than one set of Runners and Chasers may be chosen, but each Chaser must chase only his own designated Runner.

Guided Mystery Walk (#141) (all ages)

This is an excellent game to mix the ages. In fact, since the groups should not be too large, and since each group sets out at its own pace and at its own time, you could have sign-up sheets that require quotas of different age brackets to make up a team. For example, 3 people under the age of ten, 1 teenager, 1 in their 20s, and 2 over 30. A course is laid out with clues to be followed at a leisurely pace. One clue leads to the next and all receive a reward for solving the puzzle and completing the walk. A total of 8–12 clues is about the right number. Clues are posted for all to see (they could be laminated in case of inclement weather). The walk is not timed and groups may start out at any time. It works best if the groups are staggered so they are not following one another to the next location.

At the start of the Guided Walk, a sheet like the following is given to each group. This sample was laid out with clues found in Bible verses; however, other adaptions could easily be made. See the end of this explanation for other possibilities.

Sample:

Guided Mystery Walk

Clues for the next location are given in <u>underlined words</u> within the verses. Put these underlined words together to figure out where the next clue is located. Then collect the highlighted letters (one at each location) to figure out the secret message.

START

Nehemiah 7:5, "So my God put it into my heart to assemble the nobles, the officials and the common [p]eople for <u>registration</u> by families."

Genesis 4:7, "Cain was then <u>building</u> a city, and he named it after his son Enoch."

From this, the walkers would know that the next clue is somewhere near the Registration Building and the first letter of the mystery message is "P." (The "P" should be highlighted with a colored highlight pen. Above, it is bracketed.)   P _ _ _   _ _ _ _   _ _ _ _

Other examples:

Judges 9:38, "Then Zubal said to him, 'Where is your <u>big</u> talk now?'"

Genesis 12:8, "And he went toward the hills of Bethel and pitched his <u>tent</u>."

Judges 5:6, "The roads were abandoned, and the travelers took to <u>winding paths</u>....."

Numbers 22:5, "So Balak sent messengers to summon Baalam who was.....<u>near the river</u>."

II Kings 16:14, "And put it on the <u>north side</u> of the new altar."

Exodus 2:3, "She got a papyrus <u>basket</u> for him."

Isaiah 22:18, "He will roll you up like a <u>ball</u>."

(last clue) Matthew 25:23, "Well done, good and faithful servant." Come back to <u>start</u> to receive your reward.

The mystery message reads: PICK YOUR CONE

Each participant receives an ice cream cone with a choice of flavors.

Alternatives to using Bible verses could be to make up a code where strange symbols represent different letters, and a code sheet is provided to help decipher the symbols. Or have each letter represented by a number (Z=1, Y=2, etc).

Stagecoach (#142) (ages 6 to adult)

The group sits on chairs in a circle—same number of chairs as players. The reader of the story stands outside the circle. Each person is identified as one of the following characters: boy, mother, father, grandmother, cat, or dog. There can be more than one of each, depending on how many people are in the group. People are either assigned their character by the reader or draw slips of paper from a hat. When a character is mentioned in the story, the people representing that character must stand beside their chair, twirl around, and sit down again. When the word "stagecoach" is read, everyone runs for a different chair in the circle. This continues through to the end of the story.

Story: Once upon a time there was a little BOY. One day his FATHER said to his MOTHER, let's take the DOG and the CAT for a ride on the STAGECOACH. The little BOY also wanted to go but he had to stay behind to help his GRANDMOTHER. So the FATHER and the MOTHER and the DOG and the CAT all took a ride on the STAGECOACH leaving the little BOY behind to help his GRANDMOTHER. The FATHER and MOTHER and DOG and CAT were gone for a long time and the little BOY and his GRANDMOTHER become worried. Finally, they heard a rider going through town yelling, STAGECOACH!, STAGECOACH! the STAGECOACH is coming! At this the little BOY and his GRANDMOTHER ran into the street to greet the STAGECOACH. At that moment it started raining CATS and DOGS, making the situation very wet. The STAGECOACH finally pulled in and the little BOY's FATHER and MOTHER got off, followed by the DOG and the CAT. The little BOY and the GRANDMOTHER and the FATHER and the MOTHER and the DOG and the CAT all hugged each other and were glad the ride was finally over on that STAGECOACH.

My Ship Came In (#143) (ages 7 to adult)

Players are seated or standing in a circle. One of the players is the leader who knows the sequence of actions to be introduced. The leader says to the player next to him, "My ship came in." The player asks, "What did it bring?" "A fan," the leader replies and begins a fanning motion. (All motions, once started continue until the end of the game.) The player then turns to the next in line, repeats the conversation, and with his reply starts his motion. It continues around the circle this way until it gets back to the leader who introduces the next action while continuing the first. The second time around the ship brings a pair of scissors (cutting motion of index finger and middle finger of the opposite hand that is fanning). The third time is a rocking chair which means a fan, scissors and rocking motion all going at the same time. This is followed by glasses (with eyes blinking), false teeth (opening and shutting of mouth), and a hat (head wagging). You can also throw in shoes (marching while standing in place). By this time the group will be in hysterics and the game will happily end!

Murder in the Dark (#144) *(ages 6 to adult; a great teen game)*

Players are lined up, standing, all facing in one direction, side by side, eyes closed. The leader walks behind the players and chooses a murderer by tapping someone on the back once, and a detective by tapping twice. The idea here is that the identity of the murderer and the detective is a secret. The lights are turned out (by the leader) and the murderer goes to work. People go around shaking hands with each other in the dark, but when the murderer shakes a person's hand, she squeezes three times. The victim must then shake three more people's hands and then scream and die (falls down). After a certain number of people have been killed (about half the group), the leader turns on the lights and the detective tries to guess who the murderer is (the detective may or may not be one of the victims). If the detective guesses right in three guesses (or one or two, if the group is small), he becomes the leader and picks the next murderer and detective. If he doesn't guess right, the murderer is the next leader.

Spoon on a String (#145) *(ages 4 to adult)*

Divide the group into equal teams; give each team a ball of yarn with a spoon tied to one end of it. The teams line up, and at a signal, the spoon is passed down the shirt of the first person of a team, up the shirt of the next person on the team, down the shirt of the next, and so on. The last person on the team (after passing it up or down his shirt) winds up the yarn. The first team to pass the spoon and roll up the yarn wins. *Variation:* The last person, after rolling up the yarn, starts the spoon back up the line in the same manner. The first team with the spoon back to the front with the yarn rolled up wins.

Ice Melting Contest (#146) *(ages 4 to adult)*

Divide into equal teams and give each team a block of ice. At a signal, each teams tries to melt the ice without scraping or breaking it. Usual methods are rubbing it, blowing on it, putting in the sun, etc. Flame cannot be applied. After a certain amount of time (this depends on the original size of the block), the team with the smallest block wins. A bathroom scale comes in handy to determine this.

Lifesaver Relay (#147) *(ages 6 to adult)*

Divide into teams and give each person a long matchstick and each team a Lifesaver candy. The best sticks are the long, fireplace matches with the match head removed. It's important that the end of the stick is blunt (for safety) and that the diameter of the stick is small enough that two sticks can easily fit into a Lifesaver hole. Whittling may be necessary. Each player puts the stick in her mouth and the first player puts a Lifesaver on her stick. The Lifesaver is passed from person to person using the matchsticks. No hands allowed. The first team to get to the end of their line and back to the front, wins.

Tin Can Bowling (#148) *(ages 3 to adult)*

Use #2 tin cans for the pins and softballs for the bowling balls. You will need a level stretch of ground, a backdrop behind the pins, and someone to set pins. Experiment with the terrain to judge how long the alley should be. It will also depend on the age of the bowlers.

Parachute Games (#149) *(ages 4 to adult)*

Other cross-generational and noncompetative games can be organized using a large silk or nylon parachute as a prop. These may be obtained in vivid colors at game stores or may sometimes be found in army surplus stores. See Appendix C under "Dale Le Fevre" for a book on parachute games.

To use the parachute as a game prop, have all players who wish to play (may be old or young!) stand in a circle on a grassy place. Players hold the edge of the parachute with both hands at about waist level. Players may also be seated, in which case their legs are stretched out straight before them underneath the parachute. They may not peek under the parachute. One player is chosen by the leader to be "It."

"It" gets under the parachute, crawling about on hands and knees. The lightweight parachute will ripple, making it difficult to locate "It." "It" crawls about silently and tags a leg of someone holding the parachute. The person tagged must then scream and leave her place to join "It" under the parachute also becoming "It." Call a halt when there are more crawling around under the 'chute than are holding it. The game may continue by returning all players to the perimeter of the parachute and choosing some new "Its" who have not had a turn.

Earth Ball (#150) (ages 4 to adult)

Another fun activity is to rent a giant "Earth Ball," six to eight feet high which may be inflated and used as a game focus. Phone a City

Parks Department to see if one is available. Sometimes fast food outlets such as McDonalds rent them out for a nominal fee as a promotional item. Many games may be adapted or invented using this giant ball. Something as simple as dividing into two teams with each team striving to push the ball over a goal line can be a lot of fun.

ETHNIC GAMES

There could be two approaches to including ethnic games at your family gatherings. One would be to find or adapt games to emphasize your own family heritage or the heritiage of family in-laws (this is a great way to make them feel included). Another would be to simply include some games from other countries to celebrate ethnic diversity (like enjoying Chinese food if you are not Chinese). And remember, all games are ethnic to someone. Your public library will have books of games from many lands. Some of the best we've found are listed in Appendix C.

Piñatas (#151) (ages 4 to teen)

Piñatas, of course, are from Mexico. They are made of paper and come in many sizes and shapes, mostly animals. There is a small opening at the top to fill with sweets or small gifts. The piñata is hung over a limb or rafter by a sturdy wire or cord. The other end of the cord should be in the hands of an adult who raises or lowers the piñata depending on the height of the person trying to hit it. Children are lined up by height and each is blindfolded in turn and given a broom handle or other such stick to try to break the piñata with. The leader blindfolds and leads each child beneath the piñata, makes sure the others are clear, and gives the signal to start swinging. After a few healthy swings, the leader signals to stop and proceeds with the next child in line. The person controlling the cord tries to save the piñata from being broken open until at least the younger children have all had a turn. When it's finally broken open, there's a big free-for-all for all the goodies. Be sure that all edible items are wrapped for sanitation reasons. See Appendix C for a source of piñatas and goodies.

Lima y Limon (#152) ("Lime and Lemon," from Argentina)

This game is great for introducing relatives from many locations. Stand or sit in a close circle with the Fruit Picker in the center. When the Fruit Picker points to someone and says, "Lima," the person indicated must say the name of the person on her *left* before the Fruit Picker can count to ten in English or Spanish. If he says, "Limon," the person indicated must name the guest on her *right*. Should she fail, she changes places with the Fruit Picker. Continue the game as long as there is interest or until most have had a turn.

With a little imagination, it's not difficult to give a game an ethnic twist. Here are a couple of examples:

Irish Scavenger Hunt (#153) (ages 5–teen)

Divide into teams, giving team captains identical lists of items on which some green must be found. These items must be delivered to a specific location by a certain time. Items might be such things as a pop can, a shoelace, a running shoe, a ticket stub, a stuffed animal, a postage stamp, a vegetable, etc. Let your imagination run riot with up to fifty items. Lay specific ground rules: whether the team may split up to search or if all must remain together; if there are boundaries within which they must find their treasures. Other colors can be used, too, for other nationalities—especially colors in a nation's flag.

Musical Shamrocks (#154) *(an adaptation of musical chairs)*

From large sheets (22"x 28") of green construction paper or a double-fold of an ordinary daily newspaper, cut a number of shamrock

shapes—one per page. Scatter the shamrocks around the playing area. Explain that as the music is playing (Irish jigs would be great!), all players must dance or move among the shamrocks but must stay off them. When the music stops, players must rush to find a place on a shamrock. However, each shamrock must have exactly three players on it. The players on shamrocks with only one or two people are eliminated. Those who find no place are also eliminated. Remove one or several shamrocks (according to the size of the group) after each stop. Winners are the three who have not been eliminated when only one shamrock remains. The prize might be green suckers, lime popsicles, or some other such treat.

PROJECT GAMES

Projects like these are strongly recommended for family gatherings because adults and children get to work and play together.

Travois Race (#155) *(ages 5 to adult)*

Webster: "Travois (trav <u>wah</u>)—a primitive vehicle used by the Plains Indians of North America consisting of two trailing poles serving as shafts for a horse or dog and bearing a platform for a load."

This is a fun project that can include nearly everyone. Participants can develop their ingenuity, and experience teamwork and cooperation. It's best conducted in a wooded area and takes at least 4–6 hours to complete. One long afternoon or one full day is better.

Leaders need to prepare ahead of time:

1. For each team (about 10–15 per team) a pile of slender saplings or small trees (windfalls are best), trimmed of branches, 8–12 feet long. Hammers, saws, nails, heavy cord or rope, baling wire, knives, pliers.

2. Map out a lengthy course for the race, preferably up and down hills and around obstacles. Maybe flag this course with plastic ribbon.

Making the travois:

1. Groups are given material and on the word "go" from the leader, must design and build a travois sturdy enough to carry a rider over the given course. It will be used in the actual race.

2. Travois are judged for design. Prizes may be awarded.

3. Each team chooses 8 "horses" and 4 riders. (If teams are not large enough, they may exchange positions.) For our race, we made it a rule that the heaviest person in the group had to be a rider for one stage of the race. Two horses and a rider are stationed at each stop before the race begins to facilitate rapid changes.

The Race: The race begins with each travois in position and with two "horses" pulling and one rider seated on the travois. At the starting signal, the travois races to the first stop, where a change of "horses" and rider await. The change is made as rapidly as possible, and the travois continue to the second stop where the procedure is repeated, and so on around the course. The true test of the travois will be how well it withstands the race. Those not involved as horses or

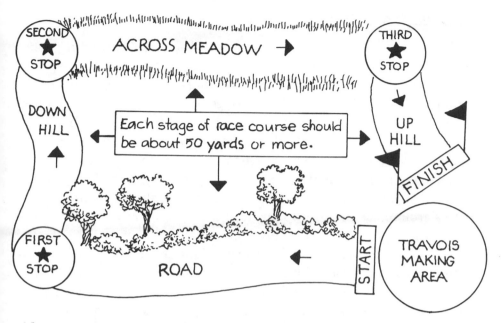

riders may want to run along to cheer but may not help the horses or riders and cannot obstruct the other teams. Grandmothers may want to stand at the finish line to cheer. Grandfathers and uncles may want to help with the design and building; some children may be riders. A great cross-generation activity!

Stilts (#156) *(ages 5 to adult)*

Making stilts and learning to walk on them is lots of fun. Prepare beforehand lengths of 2"x 2" lumber, 6–8' tall. Also have 2"x 4" pieces of wood (and screws) to attach as "platforms" for the feet. For beginner stilt walkers, the platforms should not be placed too high. Simply the fun of stilt walking is reward enough. Racing is too hazardous.

Another approach is to make *tin can stilts*. Save up soup cans or other medium-sized tin cans. Punch two holes in the bottom rim of each can, large enough to admit a stout cord or small rope. The cords are grasped tightly in each hand to hold the cans against the feet. Thus one can walk fairly rapidly but precariously.

Silhouettes of Elders (#157)

Have a special feature of silhouettes of the oldest attending member of each branch of the clan. Pin as many large sheets of paper to the wall with thumbtacks as there are branches of the clan (for example, if the reunion is of all the descendants of a particular set of great-grandparents, have the oldest living descendant of each of their children drawn). Arrange a light for projecting a shadow (a slide projector works well). Provide crayon or charcoal for the chosen artist. The subject is positioned so the shadow of her profile will fall on the paper (a seated position is usually more comfortable). The artist then traces around the profile and fills it in with crayon or charcoal. These are then labeled with the person's name and family branch and mounted on the walls. A family branch might be identified as "descendant of George," "descendant of Alice," etc. If they are quite elderly, it might be nice to save them for posterity. If they are done with charcoal and are to be stored, spray with a fixative available at art stores. If they are not preserved, be sure to take photos or videos of them.

Kite Making (#158) (ages 3 to adult)

Kite making is lots of fun and very simple but a knowledgeable leader is important. Find someone who knows how to make kites, or get a book on kite making from a hobby store or library. If no one volunteers to help make kites from scratch then buy them in kit form and put them together on the spot.

Necessary materials to make kites from scratch are thin wood laths for framing, paper, glue, string, cloth for the tail and marking pens if you want to have a design contest. Remember to allow time for the glue to dry—about 30 minutes.

PINE CONE BIRD FEEDER

Chapter 7

NATURE and ART PROJECTS

Nature and art projects work best at family gatherings and reunions that are two or three days in length or longer. And they should be scheduled toward the end of the event after the initial excitement has worn off and the participants can settle down and concentrate. Be sure to not schedule a more exciting event at the same time.

There are many projects that can employ the use of items found in nature. Children have marvelous imaginations. Give them some basic tools and supplies and they will turn out innovative crafts. On a short hike, encourage them to collect interesting pebbles, twigs, straw, leaves, pine needles, pine cones, burrs, moss, seed pods, flowers such as Queen Anne's Lace, and if you are near a beach, shells and small pieces of driftwood. Use these in the designing of various art projects.

Diorama, Peep Box (#159)

A *diorama* is a scene made in a box tipped on it's side. The bottom of the box forms the backdrop for a miniature 3-D scene. A *peep box* is made by forming the scene on the bottom of the box and a round hole about the size of a quarter is cut in one end. Another hole about 2" square is cut in one end of the lid and covered with clear or colored cellophane. When the scene is completed, the lid is replaced on the box and the scene is viewed through the peep hole. To create back-grounds, use pieces of plywood, styrofoam meat and bakery trays in various colors and shapes, construction paper, foam board, etc. Ask friends to collect shoe boxes.

To make a diorama or peep box, first sketch the scene on a piece of paper, looking over your collection of supplies for clever ideas. Blue construction

paper may be used to make a sky or it may be painted or colored. Cotton balls flattened and stretched make interesting clouds. Features might include sand for a beach, pieces of driftwood and twigs, perhaps a miniature house made of shells or popsicle sticks, a fence made of toothpicks.

Sand and Seed Pictures (#160)

Whole landscape scenarios can be created by glueing sand and seeds to a stiff background such as plywood, bristol board or foam board. Have the participants sketch a scene or assist them to do so. The scene could be of the present surroundings or of an old family homestead taken from a photo, or just make one up. Apply white glue one section at a time and attach various colored seeds or sand. Allow to dry before moving. Colored sand could be created ahead of time using food coloring. Millet, sesame, various beans, grains, rice, lentils, all make good material.

Coconut Shell Bird Feeders (#161)

Plan ahead for this one. Over a period of time have friends, neigh-bors and relatives save coconut shell halves for you. Drill three holes near the top through which you will tie string as hangers. Mix suet, stale bread crumbs, pumpkin and bird seeds, raisins, cranberries, popped corn and any other delicacies enjoyed by birds. Fill the coconut shells and hang for the birds. During the gathering, try bird watching to see which birds visit the feeders and make a group list.

Pine Cone Bird Feeders (#162)

Gather pine cones. Spread with peanut butter or a combination of peanut butter blended with lard or suet and bird seed. To be environmentally friendly, hang these in trees by string that will disintegrate rather than with wire which could be potentially dangerous to birds.

Animal Cracker Art (#163)

Enhance some of the crafts listed above by incorporating animal crackers into some of the scenes.

Rock Painting (#164)

Gather rocks with interesting shapes. Look at them from all angles. Turn them over in your hand. Maybe the shape will suggest a frog, a sleeping cat or a cliff dwelling. Pencil on the features you see and paint with watercolors. After they have thoroughly dried, the color may be preserved with spray shellack or a thin coating of white glue or whipped egg yolk carefully brushed on.

Print Making (#165–168)

If you are interested in different ways of making pictures, you'll find print making an exciting adventure. Many of the things that are familiar household items have surfaces and shapes that can be printed. By inking the object and transferring the impression onto paper you will come to discover the beautiful designs that exist in the most familiar materials. You can also make your own surfaces such as the familiar potato stamp and other techniques.

Leaf Prints (#165). Collect leaves of interesting shapes. Decide how you will arrange them on paper. When you have your design worked out, press the leaf on an inked stamp pad. Green is best but you might try other interesting colors as well. Place the leaf carefully on the paper, cover with a piece of waxed paper and press carefully with your hand. Remove the waxed paper and the leaf impression will be left on the paper. If you wish to add another color to outline the leaf, leave the leaf in place and with a sponge dipped in water color (shake excess paint off sponge before applying), outline the leaf. Allow to dry thoroughly. Cover with clear self-stick plastic (it comes in large sheets) to make a souvenir placemat to take home.

Press Prints (#166). You can use nearly anything to print with: a piece of wood, a bottlecap, screws, a rolled-up piece of corrugated cardboard, sea shells. By using all these different objects and different colors, you can make your own picture.

Materials: Collect all the different things with which you are going to print. You will also need some poster paints or tempera in different colors, a few saucers, and a good supply of white paper that easily absorbs the paint. Cover the table with newspapers.

Put some paint in a saucer (the paint must be rather thick for press printing), dip your finger into the paint and rub it lightly on the object you want to print from. Now press it firmly onto your paper, being sure not to let it slip. Lift it, and you will see the impression it has made on the paper. Try several until you get the effect you want. You may need more or less paint. In this way, try out all the different objects to see what they look like when printed. Experiment with single impressions in a row, scattered around on a page, overlapping or bunched together. Experiment with different color combinations.

When you have done this and you are familiar with the different impressions you get, you can start to arrange all those forms into a picture. It can be abstract, geometrical or an object such as a tree.

Potato Printing (#167). In potato printing, a raw potato is first cut in half and the flat, cut side of the potato is used. The design you print is made by cutting away the part on the flat surface that is not to print. The part left standing is dipped in paint and the inked potato is then applied to paper. Draw the design on the potato before beginning to cut. Children enjoy doing their own initials or using such articles as leaves that will make a pleasing and familiar design when printed.

Sponge Painting (#168). *Materials:* tempera paint; construction paper, sponges cut in small 2" pieces (cut when damp); spring-type clothespins; shallow containers (disposable pie tins); use a separate pan for each color. Children should handle the sponges by clothespins, dipping sponges in paint. Use the sponges to dab and paint a design of their choosing or draw a simple outline, such as a tree, to follow.

String Art (#169)

An attractive string art project can be made by beginning with a piece of 8 1/2" x 11" white paper glued onto a piece of 9" x 12" construction paper. This will create a colored border for your artwork. Draw a simple outline picture or use those found in coloring books. Have a choice of pictures available and prepare an example or two. First spread white glue on the outline. Then take colored yarn and lay it on the glue following the outline. The picture may be completed by following around the outline three or four times. Some interior features such as wings of birds, etc, can be outlined in shorter pieces of different colored yarn. Complete the picture by punching two holes at the top of the picture and add a matching hanger.

Tear-a-Mural (#170)

Ask a printer for some discarded paper and end rolls. Books of outdated wallpaper samples are often available from decorator shops. It's wise to ask well in advance as they may need to save one for you. Try to obtain a variety of colors, textures and shapes.

This may either be an individual project where each child makes her own picture, or a group effort. If it's a group project, you might sketch a few trees, flowers, etc, to spark their imagination. Children may have their own ideas, however, in which case allow them to have free rein. If they are making individual pictures or abstract works of art, encourage them to experiment with all kinds of sizes and shapes, *tearing* the paper to the design they desire. Don't have any scissors available. Dry wallpaper paste to be mixed with water on the spot makes an inexpensive glue. A flour-and-water paste costs even less and is easy to handle. Use popsicle sticks as applicators. Of course, one can always supply the more expensive glue sticks, if your budget allows.

Here is a home-made paste recipe that's nontoxic:
1/2 cup flour
Add cold water until mixture is as thick as cream.
Boil. Cool. Add a few drops of wintergreen to enhance the smell.

Spatter Painting (#171)

Materials: construction paper or thin cardboard; a piece of screen; an old toothbrush; water color paints or tempera paints; newspapers.

To make a silhouette spatter painting, lay out objects (such as leaves) in a pattern on paper. You can also use cut out shapes. Spatter the whole sheet of paper or perhaps just the area around the design. To spatter, hold the screen a few inches above the paper, dip the toothbrush bristles lightly in paint, and rub carefully across the screen. Too much paint on the bristles will cause blotching. You can vary the depth of color tone by the amount of paint you spatter on. A very effective design can be made by having the greatest density of color near the edges of the silhouette, shading outward with the lightest tones near the edge of the paper. When the painting is done, carefully remove the leaves or pattern that has been laid out. The result will be a white silhouette, while the rest is colored.

An interesting technique is to put all the component parts of the spatter painting on the paper (such as in a build-up). As you begin spattering, remove the pieces one at a time. Those uncovered first will be re-sprayed, causing a greater depth of color. The last pieces taken off will receive the least color.

Chapter 8   BALLOONS, BALLOONS

The beauty of balloons is that they are readily available, inexpensive, colorful and universally loved. Balloons can be used to entertain, to teach new skills, or as a game prop for numerous activities. You might even want to try your hand at inventing a new balloon game.

Be sure you have the appropriate kind of balloons for the purpose intended. Hobby stores and craft stores will carry better quality balloons than toy stores, but for some games the quality is not important and balloons for these games may be purchased anywhere.

If you intend to make balloon animals or sculptures, buy the best quality pencil balloons you can find. This way children will not be disappointed by balloons that burst too soon. Tiny water balloons are great for a harmless water fight. They burst easily upon impact.

Please remember that some balloon games cannot be played outside if it's windy.

Balloon Sculpture (#172) (any age)

This may be used an as entertainment feature for young children or as an art to be experimented with by older children and young teens. Bursting balloons can be scary for young children if the situation is not handled properly. There are numerous books that teach balloon sculpture or you may already have someone in your group who is familiar with the art. Balloon animals will be enhanced if you have a black marker on hand to add a few simple features like eyes, mouths, etc. See Appendix C for books on the subject.

Choosing Teams with Balloons (#173)

This is an elaborate way of choosing teams but it's great fun. Have the same number of balloons as you have people participating in games but have a different color and equal number of balloons for each team. For example: 32 players and 4 teams = 8 balloons of each color. Attach the balloons with tape or thumb tacks to a wooden building, large piece of cardboard or plywood. Bunch the balloons up; you want to make it easy to burst a balloon with a dart. Have a marked throwing line about 5–10 feet from the balloons.

For safety, keep all participants in back of the throwing line and make sure no one wanders in front of it. Participants are given darts to burst a balloon. The color of the burst balloon indicates the team. To speed the process, have several "balloon stations" going at one time. Late comers are assigned a team by the leader.

A simpler version (but not as much fun) is to have a mixture of inflated balloons concealed in a large garbage bag. Each player must close her eyes and choose a balloon out of the bag. The color she draws designates her team.

Get Acquainted Balloons (#174)

Prepare balloons before inflating by putting each person's name on a small slip of paper, folding the paper small and slipping it into a balloon. Folding long and narrow works best. Balloons are then inflated and used for choosing teams as above. The variation is that each person must find the person named in their balloon. Have suggested pieces of information they must learn about that person: her favorite hobby, what she dislikes most or (if she is from another part of the country), an interesting feature about her home area.

Color Balloon Game (#175) *(for ages 2–5)*

For this game you need balloons of different colors. Give each child an inflated balloon. Make up a little song that will indicate which color will stand. Example: to the tune of "Here we go 'round the mulberry bush," "This is the time for reds to stand, reds to stand, reds to stand. This is the time for reds to stand, so early in the morning." Or to the tune of "The farmer in the dell," "The blues will now stand up, the blues will now stand up, heigh-ho the derry oh, the blues will now stand up." Of course, you should be sure that each child has an opportunity to stand, but to make it more interesting and add the element of surprise, mix the colors up such as calling blue, red, green, back to red, on to orange, back to blue, or call a color for which there is no balloon. If you're outside and it's windy, attach balloons to wrists with string.

Balloon Catch (#176) *(for ages 2–5, indoors or no wind)*

Children sit in a circle on the floor or on the grass. The leader stands in the middle of the ring holding a balloon which measures from 6" to 9" in diameter when blown up. The leader throws the balloon up into the air calling the name of one of the players as it leaves her hand. The child must spring up, run into the ring, and catch the balloon before it touches the ground. To develop quickness or hasten the game, the balloon may be dropped from just above the leader's head instead of being thrown up into the air.

Simple Balloon Relays (#177–182)

(#177) Divide into teams. Each player is given a round balloon. At a starting signal, one person from each team bats her balloon through the air to the goal with her hands, then hugs the balloon to burst it (no stomping allowed!). The first person then runs back to the team, tags the next person in line who in turn repeats the procedure. The first team finished is the winner. (Ages 6 to adult)

(#178) Team members must run to the designated goal (above) with the balloon between their knees. (Ages 5 to adult)

(#179) Pass a small round balloon under chin down the line. No hands allowed! (Ages 6 to adult)

(#180) This is a "Chinese Balloon Relay." Players must carry a fairly large balloon between two sticks about 12" long around a designated goal, come back and pass it to the next person. Players cannot touch the balloons with their hands. If the balloon drops, they pick it up with the sticks and continue on from there. First team to complete wins. (Ages 6 to adult)

(#181) Each player has a balloon that's placed on the floor in front of her. She must kick it to the goal line, stomp it to break it and run back to tag the next player who is ready with his balloon placed on the floor in front of him. (Ages 4 to adult)

(#182) Each relay team has its own goal which is a chair with as many uninflated balloons on it as there are players on the team. At the starting signal, the first person runs up, blows up his balloon and bursts it by sitting on it. He runs back, tags the next person in line who follows the same procedure. (Ages 9 to adult)

Musical Balloons (#183) (ages 4 to adult, indoors or no wind)

This is a variation of musical chairs. Players stand forming a large circle facing *out*. Each player is given a paper plate to hold out in front of her. As the music plays, players pass a balloon (or there could be several going at once) by gently tossing it to the next person's plate. Any person dropping a balloon before the music stops must pick it up and replace it on her plate then pass it on. However, if the music stops while she has the balloon, she drops out of the game.

Water Balloon Toss (#184) (ages 5 to adult, outdoors)

For this one, you will not want to use the miniature water balloons that are designed to burst on impact, but a regular balloon filled with water. This might be a fun thing to do if the weather is hot and the adults are having a boring meeting. Kids are paired off and form two lines across from each other. Each pair is given a loaded water balloon. Standing fairly close to each other, the couples begin to gently toss the loaded balloon back and forth. With each toss, they move back a small step. The object is to toss gently and to keep the balloon intact as long as possible. The pair managing to throw the balloon the farthest without bursting is the winner.

The Great Balloon Battle (#185) (5 to adult, indoors or no wind)

Divide the group into four teams. Each team has balloons of one color. Each player has a balloon and a construction paper fan. Teams are stationed on four sides of a square playing area, one team on each side. At a signal, all rush toward the center of the playing field and throw the balloons up into the air. Each group tries to keep their own balloons in play and put all others out. Any balloon is out that is knocked outside the designated area or against a wall. Two or three leaders should be appointed to confiscate all balloons that are knocked out of play. The winner is the team that still has balloons in play when all others have been knocked out. The fans are used as paddles to keep one's own balloons in the air and to knock other balloons out. Only the fans can be used for this purpose, not hands.

Splat (#186) (ages 7 to adult)

Any number of people can play this game. Two people (approximately the same size) lock arms back to back. Many balloons, fully inflated, are scattered all over the floor. The balloons must be broken by sitting on them without breaking the arm lock. The pair with the most broken balloons is the winner.

Balloon Tournament (#187) (ages 8 to adult)

Choose as many couples as you like and divide into teams at opposite ends of the games area. (The couples do not need to be male/female.) One person from each couple will be a horse, the other a rider (however, the "rider" does not actually ride the horse). There will be an equal number of couples at each end. Fasten a red balloon to the back of each horse on one team and a blue balloon to the back of each horse on the other team (a safety pin works well). At the signal, the teams charge each other, attempting to burst the balloons of the other team. The horse must stay on all fours and is not allowed to participate in the bursting of the balloons. He tries to stay near his rider for protection. The riders try to protect the balloons of their horses while trying to burst the balloons of the opposing horses. A time frame may be chosen by the leader and the team with the most horses with their balloons intact is declared the winner. If all balloons on one team are broken, the other team is then declared the winner. This can also be played with couples competing (no teams). *Variation:* The rider and horse are tied to each other with cord or yarn (4–8 feet long).

Balloon Stomp (#188) *(ages 12 to adult)*

This is every person for himself. Tie an inflated balloon to each person's ankle by a long string (to avoid skinned ankle bones). The balloon should be about six inches from the ankle when resting on the floor. At the signal, each person tries to break the other's balloons by stomping on them while protecting their own. The winner is the last one with an intact balloon.

Couple Balloon Stunt (#189) *(ages 12 to adult)*

This one is as much fun for the spectators as for the participants. Prepare one large (oversized) coveralls and a garbage bag full of inflated balloons for each couple. Have each couple choose which is to wear the coveralls. At a "go" signal, one person puts on the coveralls. Then the other stuffs the balloons inside the coveralls, getting in as many as he can down the legs, etc. They *think* they are racing to see who can get the most in the fastest, and they are. But when they have finished, the stuffer is given a straightened paper clip and told they must burst the balloons through the coveralls. No poking allowed!

Swat (#190) *(ages 13 to adult)*

This game is best for the older kids. Each person has a balloon tied to their waist by a string long enough so it hangs down their back. Each person is also given a rolled up newspaper. The object is to burst, by swatting, other people's balloons, while trying to protect one's own. It is harmless but the air will resound with screams and yells. The rule of the game is that they must *only* swat the balloon but who can avoid a few misses? As above, the winner is the one who keeps her balloon intact the longest.

Super Balloon Ball (#191)

To make a super balloon ball that can be used for a number of games, fill a garbage bag with inflated balloons, making it as round as possible. Tie with a twist tie or tape. This balloon ball should not be jumped on, or climbed on, or kicked violently.

An example of a game that could be played with this ball would be to have two circles of players, one inside the other and spaced about four feet apart. The ball is tossed into the middle. The objective of the inner circle is to get the ball totally outside the circles and the objective of the outer circle is to keep it in. A *variation* that could be played would be to have the two circles of players laying on the ground with their feet in the air, using feet instead of hands to try to control the ball.

Chapter 9

FUN FOODS

The following are not intended necessarily to be full-fledged meals, although some would serve that purpose. These are more intended to be fun snacks that serve as items of entertainment, or provide refreshments for a theme party.

Mystery Balls (#192)

No heat needed! What will you find in those strangely shaped balls? They all look the same but the mystery is not solved until you take your first bite!

Needed: Large mixing bowl, large spoon, measuring cup, cookie sheet, tablespoon.

Ingredients: 1 cup peanut butter, 1 cup dry milk powder, 1/2 cup honey, 1/4 cup toasted wheat germ. Filler: raisins, whole nuts, chocolate chips, strawberries or use your imagination!

1. Put first two ingredients in a large bowl: blend well.

2. Add next two ingredients to the mixture in the bowl. Stir until batter is smooth.

3. Drop one tablespoon of the batter onto the cookie sheet. Press batter into a patty about 3 inches wide. Fill cookie sheet with patties.

4. Choose a filler and place it in the center of each pattie.

5. Fold the sides of the peanut butter patty around the filling to form a weird "ball."

6. Store in the refrigerator and eat later!

Shaggy Dogs (#193)

Put chocolate syrup and coconut in two dishes. Toast marshmallows, dip in chocolate, then in coconut. Try slightly toasting the coconut before eating. Eat from the stick. To make syrup, melt one chocolate bar with a tablespoon of milk; or mix one tablespoon cocoa mix (the sweetened kind) with one teaspoon of water.

Trail Mix (#194)

Snack food for extra energy on a hike may include any mix of ingredients you like: raisins, Cheerios, peanuts, nuts, chocolate chips, dried fruit, hickory stick potatoes or stick pretzels.

Jello Jiggler Finger Food (#195)

For each recipe, use two large boxes or four small boxes of Jello of the flavor of your choice. Thoroughly dissolve the Jello in 2 1/2 cups of boiling water or fruit juice. Pour into a 9 x 13 cake pan. Chill three hours. To remove from pan, set pan for a moment in warm water and turn out onto waxed paper. Cut into squares or, more attractively, cut into shapes with cookie cutters. This may be made ahead of time, stored between layers of waxed paper, and kept in a cooler until ready to eat.

Ice Cream Cone Cupcakes (#196)

Prepare your favorite cupcake batter. Fill flat bottomed ice cream cones to the half way mark with the batter. Place on a cookie sheet and bake. Decorate any way you please. Great refreshments for a "clown" party.

"Dirt" Pie (#197)

1 pkg chocolate instant pudding (4-serving size)
1 cup cold milk
1 qt. whipped topping
20 chocolate sandwich cookies, chopped (like Oreos)
1 1/2 cups miniature marshmallows
1, 9 inch prepared graham cracker crust
Gummy worms for decoration

Prepare pudding according to package directions, decreasing milk to one cup. Fold in whipped topping. Stir in 2/3 of the cookies and all of the marshmallows. Spoon into the crust. Sprinkle top with remaining cookies. Decorate with gummy worms. Freeze until firm, about four hours. Remove from freezer 10 minutes before serving for easy slicing. Or it may be served in a large flowerpot (remember: it looks like dirt) that has been plastic wrap lined or small individual flowerpots likewise lined. This is a real hit with children, especially if served with a gummy worm and an artificial flower stuck in the "dirt"!

Frogs on a Log (#198)

Children can prepare these snacks for themselves using plastic knives. Pre-cut celery sticks into approximately three inch pieces. Smear with peanut butter or cream cheese. Place raisins at intervals along the "log" to represent "frogs."

Peanut Butter Clay (#199)

This is a play dough kids can use to mold whatever strikes their fancy, then eat!

Mix:

1 cup peanut butter	1 1/2 cups non-fat dry milk
1 cup corn syrup	1 1/4 cups powdered sugar

Mix the four ingredients into a clay consistency. Add a little more dry milk if it seems too sticky. Give each child about one quarter cup of "clay" on a piece of waxed paper. Allow them to create anything they please. Have bowls of this clay with carrot and celery sticks, pretzel sticks, Cheerios, raisins and chocolate chips to decorate. Then let them enjoy! Makes about four cups of clay.

S'Mores (#200)

Roast marshmallows in the usual manner. Place marshmallow on a graham cracker. Place a square from a milk chocolate bar on top of the marshmallow while it is still hot. Top with a second graham cracker and smoosh to a make a "sandwich." Enjoy. You'll want s'more!!

Banana Boats (#201)

Without peeling it, slit the skin of a banana lengthwise. Tuck pieces of a plain milk chocolate bar or chocolate chips under the skin. Wrap in aluminum foil. Warm over a fire to melt the chocolate. Unwrap from foil, open the skin without removing it from the banana, and eat with a plastic spoon.

Roast Apples (#202)

Roast on a stick over hot coals, turning constantly until the skin can be peeled off with the fingers. Each guest immediately rolls hot apple in cinnamon and brown sugar. Consume!

Biscuits on a Stick (#203)

These are a good accompaniment to "Hobo Stew" or may be served as a dessert by filling the hole left by the stick with margarine and jam. Here's how you do it:

Prepare a fire as you would to roast wieners. Have packaged biscuit mix prepared as a stiff dough as suggested on the package, or use the pop-open, pre-mixed dough. Mold dough onto the ends of sticks that are 1/4" to 1/2" in diameter and about three feet long (willow works well). Make sure the dough is firmly molded onto the stick and the edge sealed so it won't fall off. Roast over the fire as you would a weiner, turning occasionally so that it cooks evenly. Slide off the stick.

Gourmet Hot Dogs (#204)

Slit a weiner lengthwise without cutting all the way through. In the slit insert pieces of cheese. Wrap the weiner in a piece of bacon wound in a spiral fashion, securing at each end with a toothpick. Roast over an open fire in the conventional manner. Serve in hot dog buns with whatever condiments you wish: chopped onion, mustard, relish, ketchup.

Hobo Stew (#205)

Each person brings one can of any food: canned meat, vegetables, soup, stew—anything suitable to go into the communal pot. All are combined. It's surprising how good this turns out to be! Don't forget the can opener and utensils!

Pocket Stew (#206) (foil wrapped individual dinners)

Have a good fire prepared ahead of time, burned down to hot coals. Also prepare ahead of time: Two squares approximately 15"x15" heavy aluminum foil for each person. Potatoes diced in 1/2 inch cubes or thinly sliced. Diced or thinly sliced carrots. Bulk hamburger, not made into patties. Chopped onion. Margarine, salt, pepper. Other vegetables and seasonings may also be added such as canned peas, corn, garlic powder.

Give each person two pieces of aluminum foil for double thickness. Place a spoonful of hamburger onto the foil without pressing it into a patty. Then layer as much potato, carrot, onion and/or other vegetables as desired. Season with salt and pepper. Fold the four corners of the foil to make a sealed package. Firmly roll the top so steam cannot escape. Place in the hot coals, turning occasionally so it does not burn. Have someone tend the fire while others play games for about 20 minutes. Each person will know his own package by the distinctive way in which he has folded his package! The food will steam in it's own juices. The flavor is out of this world. Eat the stew directly out of the aluminum foil package with spoons.

Chapter 10

PENCIL and PAPER GAMES

Most of the games in this chapter work well at banquets, immediately before or after the meal, while people are sitting around talking. However, they can certainly work well at other times, too. Try a few for mixers, quick give-away contests (the first person to answer correctly wins a prize), as team contests or just hand them out for people to finish at their leisure. They all work for rainy day activities and some are great for family newsletters, too.

Relationship Questions (#207)

Give each person a sheet of paper and have them number from 1 to 10. Then read the following questions out loud. Or just read the list and the first correct oral answer to each question wins.

1. What would your relation be to your aunt's mother's father's wife? *Answer:* She would be your great-grandmother.

2. What would your relation be to your father's uncle's brother's sister? *Answer:* She would be your great-aunt.

3. What would your relation be to your mother's nephew's daughter's

son? *Answer:* He would be your third cousin.

4. What would your relation be to your brother's son's sister's mother? *Answer:* She would be your sister-in-law.

5. What would your relation be to your sister-in-law's father-in-law's grandson? *Answer:* He would be your nephew or your son.

6. What would your relation be to your sister's father's stepson's mother? *Answer:* She would be your step-mother.

7. What would your relation be to your uncle's father's only grandchild *Answer:* That would be yourself.

8. What would your relation be to your bother-in-law's wife's grandmother's husband? *Answer:* He would be your grandfather.

9. What would your relation be to your father's father's daughter's daughter? *Answer:* She would be your first cousin (or possibly yourself).

10. What would your relation be to the granddaughter of the only son of your mother's mother-in-law? *Answer:* She would be either your niece or your daughter.

[Source: *The Cokesbury Game Book*. Copyright 1966 by Abingdon Press, Nashville, TN. Used by permission.]

"Who Am I" Sheets (#208) (ages 6–12)

Have children fill out these biographical sheets (see next page) when they arrive and post them. Children younger than 6 could be accommodated if the parents do the filling in. The sheets could be designed with spaces for photos or not, as you choose. A Polaroid camera could provide instant photos. This really helps kids get to know each other and helps adults get to know the kids. Just this little bit of information gives lots to talk about.

"Who Am I" Booklets (#209) (ages 6–12)

Take the above sheets and compile them into a booklet entitled "Kissing Cousins, Ages 6–12, 19__." The kids could take them home, they could be sold at the reunion, and they are great items for the family archives. Imagine the chortles at a reunion fifty years hence!

If your gathering or reunion lasts several days, this could be an on-

WHO AM I?

My name is _____.

You can call me _____.

I am ___ years old and in Grade ___ at school.

My address is _____.

I have ___ brothers and sisters. Their names and ages are

_____.

My parents' names are _____.

My favorite hobby is _____.

I am especially good at _____.

My favorite game is _____.

My favorite thing to eat is _____.

My favorite place to visit is _____.

I wish that I could _____.

My favorite holiday is _____.

Oh, yes, my birthday is _____.

Signed _____

Today's date is _____.

PHOTO

HERE

going project. Each child makes his own sheet. These are collected together and photocopied. A cover page is decorated and/or signed by all the children and photocopied onto colored card stock. The booklet could be prepunched to fit a 3-ring binder, stapled, or tied with ribbon. Other, fancier (and more expensive) means of binding are available at the large photocopy shops. Compilation could be by family lines, states, or ages. It could have color coded sections for each family branch. You might consider borrowing or renting a photocopy machine, but if photographs are involved, it's always best to run to a large photocopy store where they have fancy machines that do a much better job of copying photos. The booklets could be sent to elders and others unable to attend. The individual sheets could be laminated and made into place mats. Sound like work? Maybe. But if it accomplishes the purpose of building bridges to lasting family affinities, it might just be worth it.

[A special thanks to my daughter-in-law, Sharon Erickson Anderson, who uses this project with her children's choir.]

Autograph Hunting Games

These are good mixer activities that help guests become acquainted. Prepare a list like one of the samples shown below, but try to make it pertain directly to your own family. Have the list photocopied and distributed to each guest along with pencils. Each person talks to the others and tries to get at least one signature in each space or box, but only one autograph from each person. The idea is to get acquainted, not finish first. If the idea is to finish first, then some people may just try to get signatures and not take the time to sign for others.

First Name Autograph Hunt (#210)

Listed on the form below are clues that suggest first names. They do not necessarily have to apply to a specific person, but to anyone whose name fits the clue. Make up your own list and put a fill-in line where the suggestions in parentheses are now. Signatures are gathered on the proper lines. When the list is complete, it's turned in to the judges. Be sure that the autograph hunter has her own name written in the proper space. Nicknames count.

Your name: _____

Clues for names (first names or nicknames only):
1. Someone whose first name rhymes with Ted. (Ed, Red, Ned)
2. Man's name that is something to be paid. (Bill)
3. Male of the turkey family. (Tom)
4. A famous queen. (Anne, Elizabeth, Katherine)
5. Name of a saint. (Anne, Francis, Joseph, Katherine)
6. A name that suggests a beach. (Sandy)
7. A name that rhymes with a part of the foot. (Joe, Neal)
8. A name that rhymes with duck. (Chuck)
9. A name that is also a city. (Hiram, Louis, Giles, Columbus)
10. A famous beauty. (Helen)
11. A name that rhymes with whim. (Tim, Jim, Slim)
12. A Shakespearean character. (Kate, Henry, Richard)
13. A biblical name. (Amos, Ruth, Esther, John, James)
14. A double name such as Julianne. (Marianne, Annabel, Joanne)
15. A former president's name. (Remember, this must be a first name:
    Lincoln, Harrison, Wilson, Arthur)

Get Acquainted Autograph Mixer for All Ages (#211)

Here are some other quests for the autograph hunt on the next page. Or just put a fill-in line after each one and use it in this format. These are just ideas. Be creative and invent your own list.

Find the following:
1. Someone born in this State or Province.
2. Someone married within the past year
3. A parent of three or more children
4. Someone who likes to camp
5. A grandparent for the first time this year
6. Someone with a tattoo on his (her) arm
7. Someone who is a twin
8. Parent or grandparent of twins
9. Someone whose grandmother is still living
10. Someone who moved into a new house within the past year
11. Someone born on a legal holiday, Christmas or New Year's Day
12. A pipe smoker

(Continued on page 87)

I come from a family of 4 children—no more, no less.	My grandmother is still living.	My birthday is in July.
My favorite sport is skiing.	I inherited a piece of family jewelry.	I don't like liver.
I am named for an ancestor.	I was at Expo.	I've flown in a jet.
I am a twin.	I love spaghetti.	I have blue eyes.
I've been across the U.S.	I have drawn up a family tree.	I'm said to look like one of my grandparents.
I have a government job.	I was born on a Holiday.	My hobby is photography.
I was born in a foreign country.	I am a stamp collector.	I don't want to get married.
I own a motor scooter.	I have lived in at least 4 different states.	I live in a house that at least 3 consecutive generations have lived in.

(continued from page 85)

13. Someone married 10 years or more
14. Someone who lives on a farm
15. Someone who carries a lucky piece
16. Someone who drives a Ford
17. Someone in business for him/herself
18. Someone who flew to the gathering
19. Someone who is an officer in a club
20. Someone who is a war veteran (any war)
21. Someone who traveled more than 500 miles to get here

Kids' Get Acquainted Autograph Mixer (#212)

This is just like the previous autograph hunt, except for kids.

Shakespearean Romance (#213)

From this list of Shakespeare's plays, fill in the possible answer to each question below. Use each title only once.

Twelfth Night
Merry Wives of Windsor
Loves Labour Lost
The Tempest
A Comedy of ErrorsThe
All's Well That Ends Well
As You Like It
Hamlet
Midsummer Night's Dream

Anthony and Cleopatra
Merchant of Venice
Measure for Measure
Much Ado About Nothing
Two Gentlemen of Verona
Romeo and Juliet
Taming of the Shrew
Julius Caesar

1. Who were the lovers?
2. What was their courtship like?
3. What was her answer to his proposal?
4. About what time of the month were they married?
5. Of whom did he buy the ring?
6. Who were the best man and main of honour?
7. Who were the ushers?
8. Who gave the reception?
9. In what kind of place did they live?
10. What was her disposition like?
11. What was his chief occupation after marriage?
12. What caused their first quarrel?
13. What did their courtship prove to be?
14. What did their married life resemble?
15. What did they give each other?
16. What Roman ruler brought about reconciliation?
17. What did their friends say?

....

(Answers below are for the group leader only.)

1. Romeo and Juliet; 2. Midsummer Night's Dream; 3. As You Like It;
4. Twelfth Night; 5. Merchant of Venice; 6. Anthony and Cleopatra;
7. The Two Gentlemen of Verona; 8. Merry Wives of Windsor; 9. Hamlet;
10. The Tempest; 11. Taming of the Shrew; 12. Much Ado About Nothing;
13. Loves Labour Lost; 14. A Comedy of Errors; 15. Measure for Measure;
16. Julius Caesar; 17. All's Well That Ends Well.

Improbable Headlines (#214)

Each headline below describes a well-known children's story, verse or song.

1. Youngster Vanishes in Freak Storm
2. Clever Builder Outwits Sly Adversary
3. Poor Bargain Brings Ultimate Wealth
4. Hoodlum Osculates Unwilling Maidens
5. Friends Eager to Assist in Painting Project
6. Unique Individual Mortally Injured in Fall
7. Odd Pair Embarks on Ocean Voyage in Chartreuse Vessel
8. Remote Country Home Vandalized by Redhead
9. Continued Prevarication Elongates Proboscis
10. Friendless Waif Adopted by Miners
11. Youthful African/American Annihilates Feline Foes
12. Enormous Woodsman Performs Astonishing Feats
13. Browbeaten Girl Courted by Royal Heir
14. Serious Overcrowding Discovered in Unique Dwelling
15. Couple Suffering Dietary Allergies Reach Agreement
16. Two Youngsters Involved in Accident, One Sustains Injury
17. Retarded Youth Encounters Pastry Vendor
18. Musical Feline, Amused Canine Witness Lunar Leap
19. Rural Homemaker Terrorized by Sightless Rodents
20. Lovely Somnambulist Wakened by Royal Caress
21. Lengthy Tresses Aid Lovers
22. Verbose Hare Hoodwinked by Asphalt Contrivance
23. Shepherdess Proves Derelict in Duty
24. Fugitive Pair Flees in Raft
25. Elderly Housewife and Canine Pet Face Starvation

....

1. Wizard of Oz
2. Three Little Pigs
3. Jack & the Beanstalk
4. Georgie Porgie
5. Tom Sawyer
6. Humpty Dumpty
7. The Owl & the Pussycat
8. Little Red Riding Hood
9. Pinocchio
10. Snow White
11. Little Black Sambo
12. Paul Bunyan
13. Cinderella
14. Old Woman in the Shoe
15. Jack Spratt
16. Jack & Jill
17. Simple Simon
18. Hey Diddle Diddle
19. Three Blind Mice
20. Sleeping Beauty
21. Rapunzel
22. Tar Baby
23. Little Bo Peep
24. Huckberry Finn
25. Old Mother Hubbard

Historical Crosses (#215)

With a pencil, connect the person with their history.

1. Said "Give me liberty or give me death."	George Washington
2. Said "Dr. Livingstone, I presume?"	Douglas MacArthur
3. Painted The Last Supper	Mark Twain
4. Said "I do not choose to run."	Abraham Lincoln
5. Built the ark	Confucius
6. Wrote Gone with the Wind	Patrick Henry
7. Wrote Pilgrim's Progress	Calvin Coolidge
8. Was a great musical conductor	Paul Bunyan
9. Discovered America	Eli Whitney
10. Crossed the Delaware	Martin Luther
11. An American humorist and author	Henry M. Stanley
12. Said, "I came, I saw, I conquered."	Franklin D. Roosevelt
13. Invented motion pictures	Julius Caesar
14. Discovered radium	Leonardo da Vinci
15. Invented the cotton gin	Will Rogers
16. Abdicated the British throne	Noah
17. Was called the "rail splitter."	Madame Eve Curie
18. Wrote Uncle Tom's Cabin	Margaret Mitchell
19. Was a Chinese philosopher	John Hancock
20. Founded the Mohammedan religion	John Philip Sousa
21. Signed the Declaration of Independence	Thomas A. Edison
22. Strong man of the Bible	Samson
23. Was a popular Western humorist and actor	Edward VIII
24. Was afflicted with polio	Harriet Beecher Stowe
25. Leader of the Protestant Reformation	The Vikings
26. Said, "I shall return."	Mohammed

[Source: *The Cokesbury Game Book*. Copyright 1966 by Abingdon Press, Nashville, TN. Used by permission.]

Key to Historical Crosses:

1. Patrick Henry	2. Henry M. Stanley	3. Leonardo da Vinci
4. Calvin Coolidge	5. Noah	6. Margaret Mitchell
7. John Bunyan	8. John Philip Sousa	9. The Vikings
10. George Washington	11. Mark Twain	12. Julius Caesar
13. Thomas A. Edison	14. Madame Eve Curie	15. Eli Whitney
16. Edward VIII	17. Abraham Lincoln	18. Harriet Beecher Stowe
19. Confucius	20. Mohammed	21. John Hancock
22. Samson	23. Will Rogers	24. Franklin D. Roosevelt
25. Martin Luther	26. Douglas MacArthur	

Marriage Riddle (#216)

When first the marriage knot was tied, betwixt my wife and me,
My age did hers as far exceed, as three times three does three.
But when ten years and half ten years, we man and wife had been,
My age did come as near to hers, as eight does to sixteen.

What were their ages when married and after 15 years?
Answer: At marriage, man 45, wife 15; 15 yrs later, man 60, wife 30.

Statistical Treasure Hunt (#217)

Divide the group into teams with the same number of people on each team. Each team has a captain and a person to record points. Give each team a points list like the one below. It may be wise to go over the points list before the game begins so everyone understands.

Points List:

1. Counting January as 1 point, February as 2 points and so on, add up the total of birthday points for your group.

2. Counting 1 point for each state or province, give score for different number of birthplaces on your team.

3. Give total of all shoe sizes added together. (One foot only!)

4. Add your hair color score:
   brown = 1, blond = 2, black = 2, grey = 3, red = 5, white = 5.

5. Score 1 pt. for each self-made article worn or carried by teammates.

6. Add one point for each 100 miles traveled by each person on the team. (You might need a map for this one.)

7. Add the total number of children teammates have. (If husbands and wives are on same team, count their children only once.) Each child = 1 point; Twins = 5 points; Triplets = 10; Grandchildren = 3 points each; Twin grandchildren = 10 points each; Triplet grandchildren = 10 points.

8. Score one point for each college attended.

9. Score two points for each person who has a hobby he pursues regularly. If more than one hobby, score two points for each.

10. One point for each person who has traveled outside of U.S. (or home country). Count one point for each country visited.

11. Total the number of pennies teammates have in pockets or purse.

Banquet Statistics (#218)

This is a group scoring game. Totals are calculated per table. The award may be simply applause by the group or a shared prize such as a second trip to the dessert table. Have paper and a pencil available on each table.

1. Total the number of brothers and sisters the group has.
2. Total number of blue eyes.
3. Total number of players wearing glasses.
4. 10 points for each player who likes broccoli.
5. 10 points for each player over 60.
6. 10 points for each person whose birthday is this month.
7. 25 points for each person whose birthday is this week.
8. 50 points for each person whose birthday is today.
9. 10 points for each different birth city.
10. 10 points for each different birth country.
11. 10 points for each person who flew to the gathering.
12. 10 points for each person who drives a foreign (or domestic?) car.
13. 10 points for each State or Province represented.
14. 10 points for each person who has attended another family reunion.

Romances (#219)

Supply each player with pencil and paper. Ask everyone to write the statements you ask for (the ones in the first column). When the statements have been written, each player in turn reads his answers to the questions (in italics) you ask from the list. This list may be varied or enlarged upon.

1. Give a name.	*What is your lover's name?*
2. A distant place.	*Where did you meet?*
3. A number.	*How old is he/she?*
4. A length of time.	*How long have you been engaged?*
5. A reason.	*Why did you propose?*
6. A number.	*How many other proposals have you received?*
7. Yes or no.	*Is he or she conceited?*
8. A color.	*What color are his/her eyes?*
9. A size.	*What size shoe?*
10. A sum of money.	*How much will you have for spending money?*
11. A habit.	*What is your worst fault?*
12. A virtue.	*What is your redeeming virtue?*
13. A song.	*What will they play for a Wedding March?*
14. A nearby place.	*Where will the honeymoon be?*
15. A motto.	*What will be the guiding principle of your life?*

Chapter 11

PRESENTATIONS and BANQUET GAMES

Family Stories (#220)

If you have a banquet or program (for example at a reunion), you may want to ask for "popcorn" quick anecdotes—humorous stories, family legends, etc. However, you will not want people with the "gift of gab" to monopolize long periods of time. One way to handle this is to make it clear that there will be a three minute time limit. At the end of each three minute segment, a buzzer or bell will sound and their time is up. If a person goes on past the time limit, the buzzer will sound again, after one minute. Handled with humor, this method will not be offensive. Consider using an old cowbell, a teacher's school bell, or a counter dinger such as is used in retail stores.

Themes for Banquets or Programs (#221)

If you have an annual banquet or reunion, you may be looking for a way to give it a new spark. Why not incorporate a "theme," either known by all ahead of time or as a surprise feature. Something in your family history may inspire a good take-off point. An example might be the year of immigration. If your immigrant ancestor came in the year 1863 or thereabouts, he may have heard "My Grandfather's Clock" being sung in the streets. It was the "pop" song of the day. Or you might work around the theme of Stephens Foster's songs written between 1842 and 1864. You would have over 200 songs to choose from. Other themes could be the Gay Nineties, asking key people to dress accordingly—those at the registration desk, master of ceremonies, etc. Consider the modes of dress, transportation, lifestyle, and amusements of the day. Sing-alongs are always popular. Check the public library for pictorial time-lines, books on costume, transportation and lifestyle which will give you clues to what was happening in any given time in the past.

Conversation Piece (#222)

People who have married into a family may sometimes feel on the outside. This offers the opportunity for all to share something of their heritage. If there are 6–10 people at a table, go around the table and have each person tell about their most illustrious, interesting or notorious ancestor. This is discussed during the meal. As a group they are told to pick the best tale, and at a given point in the proceedings, each table has a representative briefly share one ancestor. At one gathering where this was done, there was:

—One ancestor whose great-great grandfather was a cousin to Lord Nelson.

—One had a great-grandfather who was a cousin to Zachary Taylor, President of the United States.

—One had an ancestor who was a DeHazey who came to America with LaFayette.

—One had an ancestor who came over on the Mayflower.

—One had an ancestor who was of the Swedish nobility who lost her title by marrying a commoner.

If people are seated at long tables (cafeteria style) rather than round tables, signify which people are to share tales in groups of six. Colored tape or ribbons laid on the table cloth could divide them into groups.

Toilet Paper Pull (#223)

On each table place a roll of colored or patterned toilet paper. Without being told why, the group is instructed to pass the roll around, and each person may take as much as he wishes from the roll. When every person has taken from the roll, they are told they must tell one fact or interesting piece of information about themselves for each square they have torn off. For some, this may mean only one or two things— some may have to relate 25! This may be done while they are eating.

Write a Mini-Musical (#224)

Many families have in their oral traditions stories such as three brothers who came to America. How about writing a mini-musical based on the The Three Little Pigs or the Three Billy Goats Gruff? The Great Depression could be depicted as the big bad wolf. Creative and innovative people could select tunes like "I've been Working On The Railroad" or "Yankee Doodle" and weave the story of their ancestors with a little narration and a lot of singing. Some songs might be put on song sheets or projected overhead for group participation at selected points. Costumes and props can be simple, and use of backdrops and staging optional. The possibilities are endless.

Fake Election (#225)

A fun banquet feature would be to have a fake election with chosen candidates making ridiculous promises. Political parties could be given names such as Repugnicans, Smoocrats, Digressives. Elect a family mayor, president for the year, or "representative senator." Have suggestions from the floor for a humorous political platform.

Talent Show (#226)

Have a talent show. Advertise this with your mailed out information and have "applications" at the registration desk. Limit the number of spots and the time allotted to each person, family or group. Choose a skillful M.C. who will keep the program rolling at a good pace and not be overly verbose with introductions. The enjoyment of this will depend upon if it really moves.

A rehearsed family choir featuring songs of special family interest could provide nostalgia. Examples would be U.S. Civil War songs, or songs from the era of the grandparents' courting years.

Tongue Twister Song (#227)

This is a fun song for children or adults, sung at a campfire, banquet or as a presentation. Have the words photocopied or written on a blackboard or overhead. The first verse should be sung at a slow to moderate pace. As they become familiar with the rhythm, gradually speed up each verse.

One Black Bear
(Tune: Battle Hymn of the Republic)

Verse: As one black bear backed up the bank, ⎫ *(4 times)*
          The other black bear backed down. ⎭

Refrain: Glory, glory, how peculiar *(3 times)*
          As one black bear backed up the bank,
          The other black bear backed down.

Other verses (also used at the end of each refrain):
          As one slick snake slid up the slide,
          The other slick snake slid down.

          As one black bug bled blue-black blood,
          The other black bug bled blue.

          As one pink porpoise pulled up the pole,
          The other pink porpoise pulled down.

          As one warm worm wiggled up the walk,
          The other warm worm wiggled down.

          As one flea fly flew up the flue,
          The other flea fly flew down.

(#228) This Land Ain't Your Land

(parody of "This Land is Your Land"—suitable as a solo)

Note: This song was written from a Canadian point-of-view. For people from other countries, think up verses from your own history.

First came the Norsemen, all Scandinavian
Extremely coarse men, mostly unshave-ian
They wandered inland, and called it Finland
This land that's made for you and me.

This land is your land, this land is my land.
This far from Norway, we just won't try land
The average Viking don't have much liking
For this land that's made for you and me.

The early French had extreme persistence
Despite the Indians combined resistance
With righteous feeling they started stealing
This land that's made for you and me.

This land is your land, this land is my land
This Voyageur land and Fleur-de-lis-land
Though segregated and separated
This land was made for you and me.

Next came the English and assorted henchmen
Who started fighting with all those Frenchmen
Amid that bother, they told each other
This land was made for you and me.

This land is your land, this land is my land
The Rule Britannia, Steak and Kidney Pie land
This land of Glory, of Hope and Story
This land was made for you and me.

While the French and English were busy crying
U.S. investors were quietly buying
We didn't spot it until they got it
This land that's made for you and me.

This land ain't your land, this land ain't my land
This Canada land, Pie in the Skyland
Though we bemoan it, we still don't own it
This land that's made for you and me.

Musical Wedding (#229)

Prepare photocopies of the following story, leaving blank spaces for each of the underlined song titles. Provide a copy and pencil for each guest. Read the story and have the songs played on cue by a pianist. The guest with the most correct song titles is the winner. These are all "golden oldies." You may want to substitute other titles in a few spots or leave some out or make up your own story. You may be limited by the repertoire of the pianist or by the sheet music you can provide.

It was a very <u>Lovely Evening</u> when <u>Peggy O'Neil</u> and <u>Danny Boy</u> were married <u>Down By the Old Mill Stream</u>, while <u>The Wedding March</u> was played by <u>Sweet Adeline</u>.

They were married at <u>Three O'Clock in the Morning</u>, and were attended by <u>Yankee Doodle</u> and <u>Jeanie with the Light Brown Hair</u>. On their honeymoon they sailed down the <u>Swanee River</u> and saw <u>America the Beautiful</u>, and after enjoying the view <u>On Top of Old Smoky</u>, they crossed <u>London Bridge</u>, then finally reached <u>Oklahoma</u>. After a month they rode home on <u>A Bicycle Built for Two</u>. They were met by <u>Old Black Joe</u> who drove them across the hills to their <u>Old Kentucky Home</u> where they had their first quarrel because he left her alone <u>In the Evening by the Moonlight</u> while he and <u>Billy Boy</u> were down on the corner singing <u>Hail, Hail the Gang's All Here</u>. Then <u>Peggy O'Neil</u> went back to the <u>Old Folks at Home</u> and <u>Danny Boy</u> said," I suppose "<u>It's All Over Now</u>" but he wired, "<u>I Love You Truly</u>" and she replied, "<u>Pack Up Your Troubles</u> and meet your <u>Kentucky Babe</u> in <u>Dixie</u>." He met her <u>In the Gloaming</u>, and they started back for their own <u>Home Sweet Home</u> and from that time on, life for them was one <u>Perfect Day</u> after another. Each Sunday they went to <u>The Little Brown Church in the Vale</u> and even after Father Time had sprinkled <u>Silver Threads Among the Gold</u>, their romance was just a continuation of <u>Love's Old Sweet Song</u>.

Everybody's Birthday Party (#230)

Take a trip through the year to celebrate everybody's birthday. Assign tables by birth months. If you feel there are not enough people for a particular month, combine some. (You will be assisted in planning this if you ask for birthdates of family members on the registration forms.) Each birth month table must prepare an item of entertainment to be presented during the evening. It could be preparing a song, writing a limerick, doing a charade to depict their month or preparing a brief skit. An example might be September singing "School Days, School Days, Good Old Golden Rule Days," or July singing "In the Good Old Summertime." You can let your imagination run wild on this one. Here are some suggestions:

1. Have each person bring a "white elephant" item, gift wrapped. Be sure to have some way to distinguish the giver's birth month, so that the gift is sure to end up at another table. A gift is placed at each setting, and a time for opening gifts is designated.

2. Table decorations could have some significance to the month: Valentines for February, pumpkins for October or November, snowflakes for December or January.

3. Have a group prepared to sing "A Very Happy Unbirthday to You" from the musical, Alice in Wonderland. You will be able to find it in a music store or a public library.

Rindercella (#231) *(monograph, to be read)*

Well, here is a story that will make your cresh fleep—it'll give you poose gimples! Just think of a poor little glip of a sirl, prery vetty, who, just because she had two sisty uglers, had to flop the moor, clinkel the shovers out of the stichen cove, and do all the other chasty nores while her somely histers went to a drancy bess fall. Now wasn't that a shirty dame!

Well, to make a long shory stort, this youngless hapster was chooing her dores one day, when who should suddenly appear but her gairy fodmother. Beeling fery vadly for the wetty praif, she happed her clands, said a couple of wagic merds, and in a flash, Rindercella was transformed into a bravaging reauty.

And in the courtyard stood a magnificent colden goach, made of a pipe yellow rumpkin. The gairy fodmother bid her bimb acloard and dive to the drance but that she must positively be mid by homenight. So Cellarinda bimbed acloard, and off they went in a doud of clust.

Not long after, they came to the casterful wondle where a prandsome hince was posting a harty for the teople of the pown. As Rindercella lighted from the coach, she hanked her droperchief. And the prandsome hince, who had been peeking from a widden hindow, ran out, picked it up, and the sisty uglers stood bilently sy, not cinderizing Recognella in her goyal rarments.

Well, to make a long story shill storter, the hince went absolutely pruts over the provely lincess. And, after several dours of hancing, he was aizier than crever. But at the moke of stridnight, Panderdella suddenly cinicked. As she went stairing down the long race, she flicked off one of the slass glippers she was wearing. But, of lall the uck, the prandsome hince had forgotten to ask the nincess her prame! So the next day he tied all over trown to find a lainty dady whose foot sitted the flipper. And the lady with the only fit that footed was none other than our lading leady. So she minally prairried the fince, and they happed livily after everward. And the storal of the mory is: Girls, whenever you're looking for a husband, be sure you know where to slop your dripper.

The "Ah" Stunt (#232)

Characters: Hero, heroine, thief, cop, maid, father, mother.
Prop: A large, gaudy jewel.

Prologue: The heroine is presented with a beautiful and costly jewel by her fiance. The heroine shows the jewel to her parents. Her father doesn't seem to think much of it, but her mother seems pleased. It is time for retiring and the heroine carefully puts the jewel away. A thief appears on the scene after all have gone to bed. He is about to appropriate the jewel when the maid appears on the scene and gives the alarm with an unearthly scream. The cop takes the thief in charge. The only word spoken in the play is the word "Ah."

Note: This stunt depends entirely on melodramatic action and, in particular, on voice inflection. Each "Ah" has a different meaning and must be properly expressed.

Enter maid singing: "Ah-ah-ah-ah-ah-ah-ah-ah" (to the tune of Auld Lang Syne") As she dusts she hears the approach of the heroine and her lover and gives a disgusted "Ah." Exit.

Enter hero and heroine: Seat selves on divan, sighing, "Ah!" Look in each other's eyes and both give romantic "Ah's." The hero draws a jewel case from his pocket, opens it, and offers it to the heroine. She gives a delighted "Ah!" He rises to leave. Both express disappointment that the time has come to leave by their "Ah's." He leaves followed by a sighing "Ah" from the heroine.

Enter father and mother: Heroine excitedly shows the jewel to them. Mother gives a pleased "Ah!" of admiration. Father grunts a disinterested "Ah." Parents exit and girl stands admiring jewel. Decides to put it away for the night. Places it in a jewel box. Exit. Lights low.

Thief sneaks in: Discovers jewel. Gives a satisfied "Ah." Hears approach of someone. Gives stealthy and frightened "Ah" as he attempts to hide behind a screen.

Maid enters: Sees thief. Screams "Ah!"

Family rushes in: Variety of "Ah's." Thief tries to escape but finds all exits blocked. Gasps frightened "Ah's."

Enter cop: Sees thief and emits a knowing "Ah!" Thief gives a despairing "Ah!" Cop nabs him with a satisfied "Ah!" The thief leaves with the cop, exclaiming a disgusted "Ah." The family sighs together an "Ah!" of relief.

Multi-Channel TV Stunt (#233)

Narrator: We think that multi-channel TV can always provide us with an enjoyable evening. However, this was not the case with Mr. T.V. Ize. Last week he had a restless evening trying to watch the best of three channels showing car maintenance, baking tips and infant care. This is what he saw:

Mechanic: When you started your car this morning, did it sputter until you felt like ....
Baker: a wooden spoon. Now for between the layers get a cup of raspberry jam and ....
Nurse: work it gently into the baby's skin. The baby's diapers ....
Mechanic: should be changed once a month or every 1,000 miles or if noticeably dirty. Dirty oil with shiny metallic particles ....
Baker: gives your cake that special look when spread over the icing. If you are adding vinegar to curdle the milk ....
Nurse: remember, do not feed the baby too quickly. If the baby starts gagging ....

Mechanic: pump it full of air until all the creases are out, then let the air out and blow it up again. Now take the tire and ....

Baker: cut it into little pieces and mix it into the batter, giving it that look of variety. When you get a piece of this delicious cake in your mouth ....

Mechanic: you may be tormented by the sound of grating metal. Stop your motor and put your car ....

Nurse: over your shoulder and pat it gently. Then lay your baby ....

Mechanic: in a pail of gas, rinsing until all that worn grime has disappeared leaving a shiny surface. Take the entire brake shaft and ....

Nurse: put it in the baby's mouth. This often stops the baby from crying. If your baby wakes up in the middle of the night, your first thought may be to ....

Baker: flatten it into a thin crust making designs on it with a fork. Now for filling, use ....

Mechanic: a rag soaked in cleaning fluid. This will remove all of ....

Nurse: the baby's hair. If you notice that your baby perspires a lot, especially when you ....

Baker: put it in the oven till it rises and turns brown.

Nurse: Now if the baby ....

Baker: falls ....

Mechanic: you may find the head cracked. A temporary measure is to use Stop Leak, but replacing the head is usually necessary so ....

Baker: be sure to make it in a square pan for that popular "square" look. As a finishing touch ....

Nurse: take a clean moist face cloth and gently wash your baby's neck and ....

Mechanic: the gearbox.

Hat Fashions (#234)

Good evening ladies and gentlemen. Welcome to this happy occasion.

As you know, many a male—and especially a newly married one—accuses his spouse of ruining the family budget. We are going to show how she can have all she wants (in hats, at least) without upsetting the budget, if she'll just use a dash of ingenuity.

Just imagine the boost one's ego receives in having created these works of art, so startling and eye-catching as to guarantee the immediate attention of our audience here tonight. We are fortunate in having with us a group of glamorous ladies who will model the hats they have designed for the budget-conscious woman to wear.

So, it is with the greatest of pleasure (not unmixed with apprehension) that we now present our first creation:

The Collander Model

Here is a special creation, the collander model, modeled by Miss Don't Strain Yourself from Down-the-Drain. This was to have been a surprise on the market but the secret leaked out. It is guaranteed not to be a strain to wear and is the answer to the hot weather problem. What could be more comfortable in the heat than this super air conditioning to cool the fevered brow. The stole, of course, is a must these days. The bag adds just the right touch of glamour. Notice the earrings—they will truly cut the budget.

Hat: Collander   Purse: Box grater
Earrings : Cookie cutters   Stole: Tea towel

The Cleaner Model

This little number is modeled by Miss Tide from Ajax. Lovely, is it not? Makes one think wistfully of housecleaning. Definitely no chore to look charming in this hat! The large bag is new and easy to find things in. Note the earrings—large and airy for summer. The gloves too, which incidentally come in various colors and styles, are a trend in the Easy Off line.

Hat: Soap box   Earrings : Chore Boys
Purse: Pail   Gloves : Rubber gloves

The Pie Plate Model

This sweet little hat is styled by Miss Dell K'Tesson from Pastry Place. It is also known as the flying saucer model. A most versatile number! It may be worn at many angles—off the face or tilted demurely over one eye. If you should be at an afternoon tea when it tilts too much and lands in your lap, simply place your sandwich and cake in it and go on nonchalantly drinking your tea. Note the sweet bag that she has chosen and especially her good taste in earrings. The dainty pendant, centered with flower, blends perfectly with the rest of her ensemble.

Hat: Pie plate (with rhubarb)   Earrings: Tart shells
Pendant: Pastry blender with flower   Bag: Sugar bag

The Chamber Hat

Many of you who are interested in chamber music have probably wondered how to dress correctly when attending the concerts. Well, here is your answer—the "Chamber Hat" designed by Mademoiselle Poo-Poo of Paris. Here we have a most useful little creation.

You will notice how this petite pillbox fits squarely on the head. It is not likely to be blown off by strong winds. The tote bag is large enough to carry "the pause that refreshes" and is also just right for a change when needed. The earrings are a great favorite of pin-up girls and who wouldn't like to get their teeth into that necklace! Her stole, of course, is handy in wet weather.

Hat: Chamber pot   Necklace: Teething ring
Earrings: Safety pins   Stole: Diaper
Bag: Diaper bag with bottle in it

The Bath Mat Model

Now splashing her way in is the "Bath Mat Model" designed by Miss B. Kleen. We call this the Cover Girl Hat. This style comes in lighter and darker shades, enhanced with the fragrance of flowers—definitely a cover-up hat! The matching stole is draped artfully over the shoulder. Note the purse, ready for any emergency, which is all the rage this year, and the unusual earrings—these really stop you up!

Hat: Toilet cover   Purse: Bathmat
Stole: Bath towel   Earrings: Sink plugs

The Electric Model

Now the Electric Model. You will get a great charge out of this hat worn by Miss Light of Love, fresh from Shady Lane. I can see your faces light up with interest immediately. This hat, in the new insulation white shade, may be purchased in various shapes and sizes and should be worn firmly planted on top of the head for real chic. The necklace is absolutely essential to counteract the somewhat tailored effect of the hat. The handbag can easily be carried in front or back, depending on your requirements. Note the current style in bracelets.

The corded belt completes the ensemble. Truly a brilliant success.

Hat: Lampshade
Necklace : Plug-in socket

Handbag : Heating pad
Bracelets: Christmas tree lights

The Office Model

Finally, we present the Chairman of the Board's dream secretary, Miss Steno-Graph. Efficiency is the keynote in her accessories, but fashion dictates that this young miss take note of the always-in-fashion hat which should tighten many a budget. (Let her hat fall over her face.) Note how the simple and plain purse follows the keynote of efficiency to the letter. Let me refer you to the novel earrings which should erase any doubts about our model's ability. The efficient office girl is ready for any emergency—hence, the useful as well as decorative bracelet and matching necklace.

Hat: Manila folder or large mailing envelope   Purse: File folder
Bracelet and necklace: Paper clips   Earrings: Erasers on a string

Melodrama (#235)

This skit is a guaranteed winner; no acting ability required.

The Characters: 1. Manuel, dressed in black; 2. Maggie, the fair maiden; 3. Patrick, dressed in white; 4. Zingerella, the housekeeper; 5. and 6. The curtains; 7. and 8. Hours; 9. The Sun; 10. Night.

Props: 1. Pitcher of water; 2. Podium; 3. Chalk; 4. Trading stamps or postage stamps; 5. A broom; 6. A pail; 7. A banana; 8. A whistle; 9. An iron; 10. A piece of rope; 11. Two salt shakers; 12. A large wooden match; 13. Notes; 14. Signs as follows: A. "Curtains" (2); B. "Stairs"; C. "Time"; D. "NO" written on 30 pieces of paper; E. "Hours" (2); F. "Sun"; G. "Night"

The Narrator reads the following script. The Actors pantomime the action as described in the footnotes section (numbers in parentheses).

The curtains part (1). The Sun rises (2). Our play begins.

Manuel de Populo, son of a wealthy merchant, is in his study, carefully poring over his notes (3). He stamps his feet impatiently and calls for his maid, Zingerella.

Zingerella tears down the stairs (5) and trips into the room (6). "Go fetch Maggie O'Toole," demands Manuel. Zingerella flies (7) to do her master's bidding. Time passes (8).

Manuel crosses the floor once, twice, thrice (9). At last Maggie comes sweeping into the room (10).

"For the last time, will you marry me?" insists Manuel. Maggie turns a little pale (11). "No!" she shouts. "A thousand times No!" (12).

"Then, I will have to cast you into the dungeon," says Manuel in a rage. She throws herself at his feet (13). "Oh, sir!" she pleads. "I appeal to you (14)." Haughtily he says, "Your appeal is fruitless (15)." At that, Manuel stomps out of the room (16).

Maggies flies about in a dither (17). Oh, if only Patrick would come, he would save her!

The hours pass slowly (18). Finally, Maggie takes her stand (19) and scans (20) the horizon. Suddenly she hears a whistle (21). Could it be.....?

"Maggie, it is I, my love, your Patrick!!" He enters the room and tenderly presses her hand (22). She throws him a line (23). Just at that moment, Manuel re-enters and challenges Patrick to a duel. In a fury, they assault each other (24). Finally Manuel gives up the match (25) and departs. "At last, you are mine!" says Patrick. He leads his love away into the night (26). The sun sets (27). Night falls (28). The curtains come together (29) and out play is ended.

Footnotes: (1) Two people with signs that say "Curtains" walk away from each other beginning at center of stage. (2) Person with "Sun" sign stands up. (3) He pours water from a pitcher all over some notes. (4) Licks stamps, sticks on shoes. (5) Rips down a sign that says "Stairs" and tears it up. (6) Falls down (trips). (7) Waves arms in flying motion. (8) Person holding "Time" sign walks across stage. (9) Takes chalk and makes 3 big X's on floor. (10) Sweeps with a broom. (11) Turns a pail upside down. (12) Throws papers with "NO" written on them. (13) Falls at his feet and lies there. (14) Hands him a banana peel. (15) Hands the banana peel back. (16) Stomps his feet. (17) Waves arms in flying manner. (18) Two people with "Hours" signs walk across stage. (19) Stands behind podium. (20) Hand above eyes in searching motion. (21) Patrick blows police whistle. (22) Takes iron and irons her hand. (23) Throws a rope at him. (24) Take salt shakers and sprinkle each other. (25) Hands Patrick a wooden match. (26) Bump into the person with the night sign. (27) Sun sits down. (28) "Night" falls down. (29) "Curtains" walk toward each other.

Notes

Notes

Appendix A

Using Video to Record Family History
(See Appendix C for books and instructional videos.)

I. Video Cameras—Buy or Rent?

A. Renting.
   1. Renting eliminates a large outlay of cash, and will allow you to learn the basics of video.
   2. Don't rent for the first time the same weekend of your family gathering. Take time to play with the camera and familiarize yourself with its features.
   3. Practice being steady (minimize shaking); and, in particular, panning, zooming, and using a tripod.
   4. Learn the effects of different lighting conditions, indoors and out.
   5. Take lots of footage and critique it at home on your VCR.

B. Buying.
   1. Know what you need for your own purposes. Familiarize yourself with what is available. Go to several shops before you purchase, and ask them to demonstrate the particular features of their models.
   2. Ask for a "spec sheet" that lists the features of a given model. If they don't have these available, ask them to photocopy theirs for you. Take these home, work out the features you need and compare costs.
      a.) Lux rating. The lower the lux rating (candle power needed), the less light is essential for good pictures. Most contemporary models will have a two or three lux rating, which is adequate for almost any normal situation—including artificial light in the evening, indoors. Any model with a ten lux rating or higher will be an older model on sale, and will not be satisfactory.
      b.) Fade-in/fade-out feature. All cameras will have a built-in fade to white or fade to black feature. Determine which background you prefer and choose your camera accordingly.
      c.) Macro-zoom feature. If you are preparing a video of family heirlooms, you may want to zoom in on an article as small as a finger ring.
      d.) Format. The consumer formats are 8mm, Hi-8, VHS, Super VHS and VHS-C. Super VHS and Hi-8 offer slightly higher quality. VHS and Super VHS are larger cameras. All can be viewed on a TV screen by linking the camera to the TV. All can be copied or edited onto regular VHS tape by linking the camera to a VHS recorder.

    e.) Date and time set.

    f.) Titling and being able to "scroll" titles across the screen.

    g.) Lapse-time feature will allow the camera to take one frame at intervals of 10, 30, or 60 seconds. (Great for recording sunsets!)

    h.) Audio dubbing capabilities will allow you to add commentary, music background, etc, at a later time.

    i.) A microphone on an extension line for recording interviews.

    j.) A good tripod with a smooth panning head.

    k.) An attachable light

    l.) A good carrying case.

II. Editing.

Raw video footage is seldom entertaining or even instructional. It must be edited to produce pleasing results. This means selecting video segments, copying them (in order) to another tape, adding audio such as narration and music, and adding titles. The fancy editing equipment of professionals is prohibitively expensive.

    A. Camera-to-VCR editing. This is the poor man's method but good results can be obtained with practice. See Appendix C for instructional books and videos.

    B. Storyboarding: Planning (on paper) the sequence and length of the various segments of your video.

        1. Stay within the attention span of your viewers. An interview should rarely go over 10 minutes. A location history or a multi-generation story might last 20–40 minutes. Better to have them thoroughly enjoy a short video presentation, than yawn through a boring one.

    C. Script: A written account of narration. Sample:

TIME	VISUAL	SCRIPT
0:00 – 0:30	DISTANT VIEW OF HOUSE	"WE WOULD LIKE TO TRAVEL BACK IN TIME TO THE HOMESTEAD WHERE OUR EMIGRANT ANCESTORS SETTLED......"
0:30 – 1:10	ZOOM IN ON HOUSE	"THIS IS AS WE FIND IT TODAY......"
1:10 – 1:50	ZOOM IN ON FRONT DOOR	"ETC......"

D. Titling: A visual method of introducing each segment (in written form).
1. Take videos of titles you have written out. E.g. "The End" printed on a sign board. The author used the turning of the pages in a large leather bound Bible with generation names and dates slipped in.
2. Create digitized titles with a title generator. These generators come with some cameras or can be bought separately for cameras that can accept them.

E. Audio is usually added over the top of the video after the video editing is completed. Narration is most commonly talked into a microphone as the narrator views the video. Music can be added the same way.
1. Interest will be added by changing voices if you have quotes from a journal, obituaries to read, or other items that would indicate another person than the narrator.
2. A particular musical passage or a recorded chime will help clarify changes between segments.

III. Organization.

A. Establish a file for each generation you expect to depict. Include everything in the file you intend to use to illustrate your story. Possibilities might be photos, certificates, historical material such as portraits of sovereigns, political implications such as wars, migrations, illustrations of lifestyles, etc. If this covers several centuries, changes in costume, etc, can be dramatic.

IV. Videotaping Techniques.

A. Take lots of footage. Tape is cheap.

B. Zoom into and out of close-ups (such as photos and small objects) to add drama and movement.

C. You may have to plan for several "shooting" episodes. If so, it's best to plan them for the same time of day. Consistent lighting conditions, whether daylight or artificial light, will turn out the best results.

D. If you have a script, read it as you shoot stills. This will determine how long to allow for each sequence. A few experimental shots will give you a "feel" as to whether you need 10, 15 seconds or longer periods. Experimenting with shorter sequences for practice will aid in pacing your material.

E. Setting or background. The setting or background should be simple, attractive, and uncluttered.
1. For videotaping objects, a table or other surface with a fairly plain

covering is best. Consider what will be seen in the background as well. A plain wall will make the objects stand out more clearly.

2. For interviewing a person, a comfortable setting is an easy chair with a side table and perhaps a lamp. This will enhance and not detract from the focus of attention, which is the person being interviewed. Avoid a "busy" setting with mixed patterns or a cluttered background that will detract from the personality and content of your project. Also be careful of rocking chairs. They might put your interviewee at ease, but the action of rocking may be a distraction to the viewer.

IV. Creating Family Documentaries.

  A. Videotaping heirlooms.

    1. Gather the family treasures. This may mean contacting other family members to ask for a loan of certain artifacts, if they are willing to share them with you. You may have to take your camera to selected locations.

    2. To help introduce the origin of the heirlooms, include video shots of photos that are contemporary with the heirlooms. These could be old family photos (which are heirlooms in themselves) or photos from old books or photo archives.

  B. Videotaping a location history.

    1. If a house or piece of property has been inherited and passed down through generations, a fascinating history could be prepared using pictures, land records and commentary on significant events that had transpired there. Pictures of the house, the one-room school, the people, the place where they swam in the creek, photographs from old books of transportation conveyances, can make the lifestyle of former days become reality.

    2. There are companies that will research farms, villages and family homes in the "old country" and do a photo package for you. This obviously would involve a financial outlay, but you could use these to make your own video story. Advertisements for such companies can be found in journals and magazines such as *Ancestry* or *Genealogical Helper* (see Appendix C).

  C. Videotaping memoirs, diary or journal entries.

    1. Written accounts may have been passed down from previous generations. A narration (reading) of these accounts would make great audio to go along with the video of photos and memorabilia. Always identify the author.

D. Interviewing relatives.

    1. If you are interviewing older relatives, remember to not wear them out. *Think through* what you consider to be the most important information, and prepare to ask those questions first. Design questions using Kipling's "six trusty serving men": what, where, when, how, why, who. Try to avoid dead-end questions that can be answered with a simple "yes" or "no," unless they will elicit further information.

    2. Use "memory prompters" such as photos and memorabilia that may spark recollection.

    3. Don't neglect to record the impressions of younger people as well. A young person's recollection of a deceased grandparent may bring a totally different perspective to the personality of that relative.

VI. Videotaping at Family Gatherings.

A. Take establishing shots. These are an overview of the premises. Take shots of the building or outdoor area from across the street or from rooftops. Zoom in and out and use a tripod. Establishing shots are good for introductions to segments and for backdrops for titles.

B. Take mid-range shots of activities.

C. Take close-ups of activities and especially of everyone's face. Don't leave anyone out.

D. Get a group of siblings together to discuss what it was like at home. Remember, if one person dominates the conversation and goes on at great length, you may have to be prepared to interject with some questions the others would answer, or actually name the person you would like to respond. Be prepared too, to do some serious editing later.

E. Take portraits of each family unity or group. If you have a "family tree," take each grouping in sequence. For example: if there are eight children in the original immigrant's family, take the descendants in order from the oldest to the youngest child in the original family.

VII. Making Copies.

A. Most people will want the VHS format. If your camera is VHS, copy from your camera to the VCR.

B. For more copies, borrow or rent a second VCR and copy VCR-to-VCR.

C. For many copies, have it done professionally.

Appendix B

Beginning Genealogy

A family gathering is an ideal time to begin collecting and organizing the story of your family and put it on paper or computer. There are standard procedures and forms that have been developed over the years by family historians and genealogists to assist you in this task. If you learn to use these simple forms, your family story will come together in an organized and understandable way. See Appendix C for books, forms, and other resources.

I. Forms to Use.

    A. Your family history should always include three basic records:
        1. *Ancestor Charts* (or pedigree charts) will give you an over-all view of each family line you record.
        2. *Family Group Sheets* will give you both a summary of your ancestral lines, and details of each family unit.
        3. *Logs* will help you keep tabs on your progress, and help you decide the next step in your search.
           a.) A research log which will record the sources you have consulted or from which you have received information.
           b.) A correspondence log.

    B. Record your family history in a permanent, convenient and orderly manner. Since your family history will grow more than you realize, looseleaf binders and/or file folders and matching forms are a wise investment.

II. Ancestor Charts.

    A. This is a simple form for recording the parents, grandparents and great-grandparents of an individual. It is an important aid in placing your ancestors in time-frames and places. As with any science, work from the known to the unknown. Document every piece of information as soon as possible. Begin with yourself.

B. Here is a simple numbering system: You are #1 on Ancestor Chart #1. Your father is #2, your mother #3, etc. (Note: males will always be even numbers, females will be odd numbered. The exception is number one, which could be either gender.) Continue the ancestor charts and indicate under the right-hand names on the chart where that particular line continues. For example, on a 5-generation chart, #16 on Chart #1 is in #1 space on Chart #2. #17 may be #1 on Chart #3, etc. Simply number the chart a family line continues on, and keep them filed according to consecutive numbers.

C. Each generation back in time will be *double* the preceding generation for males, double plus one for females. In this way it is always possible to project and determine the number of even a 10th great-grandparent in a particular line.

D. Follow this procedure to fill out the chart:
   1. Print names in pencil on your ancestor chart until confirmed by documentation (birth, death certificates, etc).
   2. Print dates in this manner: 21 Sept. 1984 (day) (month) (year) Always print the date in full, e.g. 1984, not '84. You will soon be working back to another century! If the date is uncertain, put in parentheses thus: (ca. 1844). "Ca." means approximately.
   3. Print Christian or given names in lower case letters, surnames in CAPITAL LETTERS or underline the surname. All uncommon first names should be underlined if they are unusual such as Evelyn or Beverly for a boy, or Georgie for a girl, to indicate that they are not a mistake on your part. If nicknames are included, put nicknames in parentheses and quotations thus: John ("Jack").
   4. For place names, use *three* designations: e.g. Wells, Somerset, England; Plymouth, Juneau Co., Wisconsin. Define the location as clearly as possible. London could be Ontario or England.
   5. Use full maiden names for females, *not* married names. If the maiden name is not known, leave it blank and follow with a question mark thus: Elizabeth (?). If there is an unusual circumstance such as two people marrying with the same surname (e.g. Adrienne ANDERSON m. William ANDERSON), underline her surname to indicate that it is not an error. Make a note under "notations" to explain that it is not an error.

III. Family Group Records.

   A. Record information on the Family Group Records using the same principles as on your Ancestor Charts. Make a Family Group Record for each marriage and include the children from that union. If a great-grandfather married five times, fill out a sheet for each of the marriages. Fill in a separate sheet even if there were no children from that particular union.

B. If there were other marriages for either husband or wife, this should be indicated on the Family Group Record under "notations."

C. Children should be listed first born to last born. Indicate whether male or female and list all possible information on each child. If there are twins, adoptions, step-children or stillborn, place this information in parentheses after, or directly under, the child's name.

D. Place an "x" or "*" in the left hand margin next to the number of the child who is your direct ancestor. It is wise to indicate this in red for quick visual reference.

E. If you have a file folder for each person in your research, color coding is helpful. You might have a separate color for each grandparent, and the preceding progenitors in that line would follow the same color. Colored file folders are available at all stationers.

IV. Searching.

A. Begin with a thorough home search. Check for family Bibles, old letters, journals, diaries, scrapbooks, autograph books, birthday books, biographies, copies of vital records (birth, marriage, death), newspaper clippings, obituaries, school records, military records, memorial cards or funeral leaflets, wills, account books, deeds and land records. See home source search list for a more complete list.

B. After you have made your home search, you will want to expand your research into other records of genealogical value. Many of these are available through local Family History Libraries (L.D.S. Church). You may also want to visit or write to local courthouses, libraries, archives, cemeteries and historical societies.

C. Write to relatives. Send a Family Group Sheet of Ancestor Chart. If the relatives are quite elderly, make out a simple questionnaire with a *few* questions such as "Do you remember the day you moved to the farm?" "Did your father have brothers and sisters? Were they older or younger than he?" Leave space between the questions for them to record answers. Enclose a self addressed, stamped envelope for return. Many old people upon seeing a complicated form will simply shelve it until "later." Ask for the names and addresses of other relatives who have information. You might also follow up with a phone call. If you receive information, explore with further questions.

D. Collecting information at family gatherings:

    1. Fill in the information you have on each family unit as accurately as possible, and have these forms alphabetized and available at the next gathering. Ask people to take a moment to verify, correct or add to the information. Have a work space and pencils available.

    2. At the gathering, if there are some branches of the family not represented, other family members (a sibling or cousin) may have some of the requested information.

    3. Ask people to write down the names of anyone who might have information and could be contacted.

E. Be sure to log the sources you search, whether successful or not.

Appendix C

A Listing of Useful Resources for Reunion Planners
(Books, videos, and Web addresses are in *italics*.)

◆ AWARDS

Humorous—
• Funny Side Up, PO Box 2800, North Wales, PA 19454, 215/361-5142. A good source of inexpensive joke awards. However, in recent years their catalog has had some items of poor taste. Be forewarned. Free catalog.

Recognition—
• Emblem and Badge Co, Providence, Rhode Island, 401/331-5444. Inexpensive recognition awards and plaques. *www.recognition.com*

◆ COATS of ARMS

• Originally worn into battle to distinguish friend from foe, coats of arms can add much to the pride and lore of any family. To research a crest or to have a new one created, contact: The Ship's Chandler, Wilmington, VT 05363, 800/375-9469. Lots of options are available, from a simple hand-painted crest to a 3-dimensional wall shield to a blazer patch, rubber stamps or signet ring. Free catalog.

• *Design Your Own Coat of Arms* by Rosemary Chorzempa. Dover.

◆ CONFERENCES, CLASSES, CONSULTANTS

• Family Reunion Institute, School of Social Administration, Ritter Hall Annex, Temple University, Philadelphia, PA 19122, 215/204-6244. Sponsors an African-American Family Reunion Conference. This is by far the most serious family reunion conference in the U.S. to date. Everyone welcome. Founded by Dr. Ione Vargus, Professor Emeritus, Temple University.

• Myra Quick has taught a family reunion planning class since 1990 through the Continuing Education Department of the University of Memphis. She can be reached at her office at the University of Memphis, 901/678-4030.

• Matt Figi is an experienced genealogist and teaches classes in northwest Indiana on the subjects of beginning genealogy, writing a family history, and reunion planning. He can be reached at 219/924-0947.

• Reunion planning consultant. William Griffin, PO Box 521, Marlboro, MA 01752, 508/485-0424. *bgriffin@ultranet.com* Bill has lots of experience with family and school reunions.

◆ DECORATIONS and TABLE SETTINGS

• Paradise Products, PO Box 568, El Cerrito, CA 94530, 510/524-8300. Theme, ethnic and holiday table settings and party supplies. Miniature flags of many countries, table fringes, crepe paper decorations, paper tabletop rolls in many colors. National anthems of many countries on cassette tape. Roll-type numbered tickets. Also spell out your own family name with Make-A-Banner. Lots more. Free catalog.

• B. Palmer Sales Co, PO Box 850247, Mesquite, TX 75185, 800/888-3087, 214/288-1026. Good prices on piñatas, piñata goodies, and crepe streamers.

• Party goods and decorations: *www.beistle.com/*

• Custom piñatas: *www.pinatadesign.com/*

• Inexpensive piñatas: *www.delightfulthings.com/wizzeo.html*

◆ DOCUMENTING FAMILY MEMORIES

Interviewing and Oral History—

• *Oral History for the Local Historical Society*, and *Transcribing and Editing Oral History*, both by W. Baum. These books explain how to interview and how to transcribe, index, store, and present oral history tapes. Sage Publications, 2455 Teller Rd, Thousand Oaks, CA 91320, 805/499-9774.

• *Instant Oral Biographies: How to tape record, video or film your life stories* by W. Zimmerman. Guarionex Press, 201 W. 77th St, New York, NY 10024, 212/724-5259.

• *Keeping Family Stories Alive* by Vera Rosenbluth. An excellent book on how to interview family members on audio tape or video tape. Order from Hartley and Marks Publishing, PO Box 147, Point Roberts, WA 98281, 604/739-1771.

Photography—

• Seattle FilmWorks, 1260 16th Ave. W, Seattle, WA 98119, 800/345-6967. Quality film processing. Receive back slides, prints, or photos on disk (or any combination) or download your photos from the Internet. *www.filmworks.com*

Publishing Family Histories—

• Family History Publishers, 845 S. Main St, Bountiful, UT 84010, 801/295-7490. This company specializes in processing family histories into any desired form and then publishing them into the desired size, cover, and quantity. Send for their free brochure, *How to Prepare Your Family History and How to Get It Published.*

• *The Complete Guide to Self-Publishing* by Tom & Marilyn Ross. Writers Digest Books. 800/289-0963.

• *Writing Family Histories and Memoirs* by K. Polking. Betterway. 800/289-0963.

Scrapbooks and Photo Albums—

• All reunion groups should keep photo albums and scrapbooks. For a truly BIG scrapbook (25" x 20") of archival quality (that means it will still be around in 200 years), contact Scrapbook Partners, 419 N. Larchmont Blvd. #21, Los Angeles, CA 90004. 888/904-1016. This company also has hard-to-find scrapbook desks. *http://mall.scrapbooking.com/*

• Exposures, PO Box 3615, Oshkosh, WI 54903, 800/222-4947. This company has a good selection, including an Oversize Scrapbook. Free catalog. *www.pdnpix.com*

• Enduring Memories, 7 Dogwood Ln, Willow Street, PA 17584, 717/464-0963. Albums, scrapbooks and supplies. Acid-free, archival quality. Photo labeling pencils. Free catalog.

• *Family Memories* by S. McNeill and L. Stiles, Betterway Books. Inspires readers to create family albums. Hundreds of ideas on how to organize and decorate scrapbook pages. Full-color. Order from 800/289-0963.

Time Capsules—

• Time capsules are a great way to introduce yourself (and this generation) to future generations. They can be buried or placed on a mantle. Items to include are stamps, coins, paper money, a letter to great-great-grandchildren, photos, etc. Order from Erie Landmark Co, 14110 Sullyfield Circle, Chantilly, VA 20151-1615, 800/874-7848.

• Jack Mallory serves as a consultant and source of time capsules—any use and any price. Contact him at 12258 Kirkdale Dr, Saratoga, CA 95070, 408/252-7447.

• *Make Your Own Time Capsule* by Steven Caney. Workman Publications.

Tombstone Rubbings—
• How to do tombstone rubbings: *www.firstct.com/fv/t_stn1.html*

Videography—
• *Gift of Heritage.* An award-winning instructional video from Mary Lou Productions, PO Box 17233, Minneapolis, MN 55417, 800/224-8511. Explains simple video techniques that will allow you to effectively tell your family story on video.

• *Basic Camcorder Guide* by S. Bryant. Everything you need to know to get started and have fun. Amhurst Media, 155 Rano St #300, Buffalo, NY 14207, 800/622-3278.

• *Video Family History* by D. and P. Sturm. Published by Ancestry, PO Box 476, Salt Lake City, Utah, 84110, 800/531-1790.

• *Family Treasures: Videotaping Your Family History* by S. Bannister. Explains about equipment, technique and interviewing. Genealogical Publishing, 800/296-6687.

◆ **FAMILY ASSOCIATIONS**

• *Family Associations: Organization and Management.* This book tells you exactly why and how to go about forming a family association. See page 129 to order.

• *The Directory of Family Associations.* Genealogical Publishing, 1001 N. Calvert St, Baltimore, MD 21202, 800/296-6687.

◆ **FINDING PEOPLE**

• *Find Anyone Fast* by R. Johnson and Debra Johnson Knox; *How to Locate Anyone Who Is or Has Been in the Military* by R. Johnson; *Checking Out Lawyers* by Don Ray. Great books by the leading authorities on finding people. Order from 800/937-2133.

• *Get the Facts on Anyone* by Dennis King. Prentice Hall/Macmillan, NY. One of the best books available on how to do background checking. 800/428-5331.

• CD-ROMs: *PhoneDisc* and *Select Phone*, both from American Business Information, 5711 S. 86 Circle, Omaha, NE 68127. 800/284-8353 or 800/992-3766. Windows or Mac. These CDs are available in most libraries. As of 1998, the information on these two CD sets is identical but the software interface is different. In the future, they will probably be combined into one product.

• Cyberdix Investigative Services, 419 Oak St, Roseville, CA 95678, 800/788-4895. This company will check a name or a roster of names against its many databases very cheaply. *www.cyberdix.com*

◆ **FOOD**

• *Cooking for a Big Family & Large Groups* by M. Meredith. Countrywoman's Press.
• *The Black Family Reunion Cookbook.* Published by Wimmer Companies, 800/727-1034. Has a great design that can be an example for other cookbooks.

• *Family Reunion Potluck* by Carol McGarvey. Sta-Kris, PO Box 1131, Marshalltown, IA 50158. 515/753-4139. Has many good potluck recipes.

• BBQ information: *www.cyber-kitchen.com/pgbbq.htm*

• More BBQ information: *www.ces.uga.edu/pubcd/b1039-w.html*

◆ FUNDRAISING ITEMS

Personalized calendars—
• Daily Memories, RD #1, Box 69R, Bear Lake, PA 16412, 814/489-3123. This company creates a personalized calendar with up to 4 special events per day (birthdays, anniversaries, etc) and a new photo for each month.

Cookbooks—
The following printing companies specialize in creating cookbooks for fund-raisers and have how-to instructions available:

• Walter's Publishing, 215 5th Ave SE, Waseca, MN 56093, 800/447-3274, 507/835-3691. Send for free fund-raising kit. *www.custom-cookbook.com*

• Cookbook Publishers, PO Box 15920, Lenexa, KS 66285, 800/227-7282. Send for their free cookbook kit and price list. *www.cookbookpublishers.com*

• Brennan Printing, 100 Main St, Deep River, IA 52222, 800/448-3740, 515/595-2000. Send for free sample and kit.

Roll Tickets—
• Paradise Products, PO Box 568, El Cerrito, CA 94530, 510/524-8300.

Lottery tickets—
• Scratch-It Promotions, 1763 Barnum Ave, Bridgeport, CT 06610, 800/966-9467, 203/367-5377. This company has scratcher tickets (generic or custom-made) and scratcher disks that you can apply to your own tickets. Invent your own scratcher fund-raiser or ask for ideas. Rush service is available.

◆ GAMES and ACTIVITIES

• Animal Town, PO Box 485, Healdsburg, CA 95448, 800/445-8642, ask for their free catalog. Lots of great board games for kids and families, face painting kit, tapes, puzzles, many great books including: *Co-operative Sports & Games Book* (Vols. 1 & 2), *Festivals, Family and Food*, and much more.

• Chinaberry Book Service, 2780 via Orange Way #B, Spring Valley, CA 91978, 800/776-2242. Books and music for children and families. Free catalog.

• *Questions and Ancestors*. A game to celebrate your family and to share discoveries with each other. Order from Conestoga Book Service, Box 7, West Willow, PA, 17583, 717/464-0963.

• *Lifestories*. A fun board game that gets participants talking about their past. Both young and old have such experiences which makes this a great game for mixing the ages. See page 128.

• Dale Le Fevre, PO Box 1641, Mendocino, CA 95460, 707/937-3337. Dale is the guru of noncompetitive and co-operative games. His books are *New Games for the Whole Family* and *Parachute Games*. His videos are *The New Games Video, New Games from*

Around the World, Sunny Day Games, Rainy Day Games, New Soccer, and *Cooperative Group Games.* He's on the Web at *www.mcn.org/a/newgames/*

• National Association for the Preservation and Perpetuation of Storytelling (NAPPS), 116 W. Main St, Jonesborough, TN 37659, 800/525-4514. This association can put you in touch with a professional storyteller near you. *www.storeynet.org*

• Youth Specialties, PO Box 668, Holmes, PA 19043, 800/776-8008. This company has truly great books on games, skits and entertainment ideas for kids of all ages. Their *Ideas Combo* series runs from #1–53 with over 3500 ideas listed, but get the *Ideas Combo Index* first to determine which Combo you want. Also check out *The Greatest Skits on Earth*, Volumes 1 and 2. Free catalog has lots more.

• *Decorative T-Shirts & Sweats Made Easy* by Susan Figliulo. Signet.

• *The Ultimate T-Shirt Book: Creating Your Own Unique Designs* by D. Morgenthal. Lark Books.

• EDC Publications, 10302 E. 55th Place, Tulsa, OK 74146, 800/475-4522. This company has *Decorating T-Shirts* (comes with paints). Highly recommended. Catalog is $2, refunded with first purchase.

• *Painting Faces* by S. Haldine. Penguin USA, 800/526-0275.

• *Balloon Hats and Accessories* by A. Hsu-Flanders. NTC/Contemporary Publishing, 4255 W. Touhy Ave, Lincolnwood, IL 60646, 800/323-4900. How to make hats and other items from pencil balloons. Comes with balloons and small pump.

• Klutz Press, 455 Portage Ave, Palo Alto, CA 94306, 800/558-8944. This company has lots of great books that explain how to do fun things and the necessary equipment or props comes with the book. Here are two good ones: *The Unbelievable Bubble Book* by J. Cassidy shows how to make huge bubbles (necessary equipment included); *Face Painting* comes with paints. Free catalog.

• Personalized crossword puzzles to dress up your next newsletter or flyer. $20 each. See page 126. Reunion Research, 3145 Geary Blvd #14, San Francisco, CA 94118.

Toasts—

• *Toasts: Over 1500 of the best toasts, sentiments, blessings and graces* by P. Dickson. Crown Publishers.

• Virtual toasts: *www.thevirtualbar.com/~willie/Toasts/*

◆ GENEALOGY

• *www.CyndisList.com* This Web site lists over 20,000 sites that are genealogy and reunion oriented. It is very comprehensive and up to date. A great resource.

• *The Complete Idiot's Guide to Genealogy* by C. Rose and K. Ingalls. Alpha Books.

• *Unpuzzling Your Past: A basic guide to genealogy* by A. Croom. Betterway Books. 800/289-0963.

• Genealogy forms such as Family Group Sheets and Ancestor Charts can be purchased from Ancestry (800/531-1790) or Everton Publishers (800/443-6325).

• *Genealogical Helper Magazine*, Everton Publishers, PO Box 368, Logan, UT 84323, 800/443-6325. Six issues per year for $24, over 285 pages per issue—a real bargain. It will put you in direct contact with things genealogical. Many ads on helpful books, videos, T-shirt companies, family history printers, etc.

• *The Family Tree*. A newspaper focusing on genealogy of the British Isles but includes other countries, too. *The Family Tree*, Odom Library, Moultrie Public Library, PO Box 2828, Moultrie, GA 31776-2828. Has an annual newsletter contest. Published bi-monthly for postage contributions.

• *Heritage Quest Magazine*, PO Box 329, Bountiful, UT 84011, 801/298-5446. A genealogy magazine & mail-order bookstore and lending library.

• *The Researcher's Guide to American Genealogy* by V. Greenwood. Genealogical Publishing Co, 1001 Calvert St, Baltimore, MD 21202, 800/296-6687.

• *Kinship: It's All Relative* by J. Arnold. Explains everything there is to know about kinship. From Genealogical Publishing, see above.

• Board for Certification of Genealogists, PO Box 5816, Falmouth, VA 22403. To locate a professional genealogist near you, write for their Roster of Certified Persons. There is a small charge.

• National Genealogical Society, 4527 17th St. N, Arlington, VA 22207-2399, 703/525-0050. This is a membership society that offers annual conventions, a mail-order lending library, a home-study course, and many books, forms and resources. To find someone near you who can speak to your group on the subject of genealogy or local history, get their *Speaker's Directory*.

• The Family History Library of the LDS Church, 35 N. West Temple St, Salt Lake City, UT 84150, houses the most extensive collection of genealogical information in the world. Documents from around the world have been microfilmed and are available for inspection. The library is open every day except Sunday and holidays. The library information number is 801/240-2331.

The LDS Church also has over 2000 Family History Centers located throughout the world. These Centers are small repositories that are linked to the main library in Salt Lake City, and are good places for beginners to learn about genealogy. Look in the white pages of your phone book under Church of Jesus Christ of Latter Day Saints, then under that title look for genealogy library or Family History Center. Or write to the main library in Salt Lake City (address above).

Genealogy for Kids—

• *Genealogy*, a Merit Badge Series pamphlet from the Boy Scouts. A good resource that anyone can order. 800/323-0732.

• *Roots for Kids* by Susan Beller, Genealogical Publishing Co, 800/296-6687.

◆ HISTORICAL PRINTOUTS

• Window In Time, 4321 Laurelwood Way, Sacramento, CA 95864. Send a date and get a computer printout of the history and other trivia of that time; a real value at $8 per printout (1998). Especially good for 50th wedding anniversaries. Prices may change. For the current price, send a stamped self-addressed envelope to the above address.

◆ INTERNET (see other Web sites listed throughout this section)

• *www.CyndisList.com* This Web site lists over 20,000 sites that are genealogy and reunion oriented. It is very comprehensive and up to date. A great resource.

Family Web Pages—

• *Home Sweet Home Page* by R. Williams. Peachpit Press. A great book on how and why to create family Web pages. 800/283-9444.

• A beautiful family web page: *www.surnames.com/organizations/peacock/*

◆ MEDICAL HISTORY

• March of Dimes, National Office, 1275 Mamaroneck Ave, White Plains, NY 10605, 914/428-7100, or contact your local chapter, listed in the white pages of your phone book. Ask for their free pamphlet, *Genetic Counseling.*

• *Family Medical Census Kit* by A. Anderson. This kit gives you all the information and forms necessary to conduct a survey of genetic diseases and medical problems within your family. Genealogy Plus, PO Box 69, Langdon, Alberta, T0J 1X0, Canada.

◆ MERCHANDISE

• Quality marble paperweights make great take-home gifts. You can incorporate your family crest into the design. Order from Paperweights, Ltd, 3661 Horseblock Rd, Unit O, Medford, NY 11763, 516/345-0752.

• Preserve a precious photo in needlepoint or cross-stitch. Custom chart made from original photo. Designs by Karen, PO Box 65490, Vancouver, WA 98665-0017, 360/694-6881.

• Button making machines: Badge-A-Minit, PO Box 800, LaSalle, IL 61301, 800/223-4103. *www.badgeaminit.com/*

• Reunion t-shirts with images of old photos: *www.bowplus.com/reunion.html*

◆ NEWSLETTERS and MAILERS

• *Creating Family Newsletters* by Elaine Floyd. A unique book by the foremost authority on creating newsletters; covers the whole gamut from hand-crafted to computer-generated newsletters. Highly recommended. Order from 800/289-0963. Also check Elaine's Website at *www.newsletterinfo.com.*

• *Editing Your Newsletter* by M. Beach. Newsletters and mailers are often what sells a reunion. This is one of the best books on the subject. Order from 800/289-0963.

◆ REUNION SITES

• *Campus Lodging Guide.* Updated yearly. Listing of inexpensive lodging, campus accommodations, YMCA centers, home exchanges, much more. B&J Publications, PO Box 5486, Fullerton, CA 92838, 800/525-6633. *www.campus-lodging.com*

• *The Best Bargain Family Vacations in the U.S.* by L. Sutherland. St. Martins Press. 200+ destinations: state parks, resorts, beaches, historical and cultural sites, learning vacations. All kid-friendly.

• *Super Family Vacations: Resort and Adventure Guide* by M. Shirk and N. Klepper, HarperCollins, New York. Excellent, highly recommended.

• *Ranch Vacations* by Eugene Kilgore. Lists over 200 guest ranches in the U.S. and Canada, and includes information on children's programs, rates, and nearby attractions. John Muir Publications, PO Box 613, Santa Fe, NM 87504, 800/888-7504.

• Gene Kilgore's dude ranch Web site: *www.ranchweb.com*

• Dude Rancher's Association, PO Box 471, LaPorte, CO 80535, 970/223-8440. *www.duderanch.org*

• *Dude Ranches of the West* by J. Franklin. Homestead Publishing.

• *Floating Vacations* by M. White. A great book but out of print. Try your library.

• Travel books and maps: *www.randmcnallystore.com*

• Houseboat Association of America, 4940 N. Rhett Ave, Charleston, SC 29405, 803/744-6581. Send $3 for a listing of houseboat rental companies in North America.

◆ **SOFTWARE**

• *Reunion* from Leister Productions, PO Box 289, Mechanicsburg, PA 17055, 717/697-1378. *www.LeisterPro.com*

• *Family Tree Maker* by Broderbund Software, PO Box 6125, Novato, CA 94948, 415/382-4770. *www.familytreemaker.com*

◆ **STATIONERY**

• Quill Corp, 100 S. Schelter Rd, Lincolnshire, IL 60197-4700. Imprinted and plain envelopes; file card trays, metal or plastic, 3 sizes; file cards, 3 sizes, lined or plain and in 6 colors plus white; address labels.

• Walter Drake and Sons, Colorado Springs, CO 80940 (that's all the address you need). Return address labels, and imprinted envelopes in quantities of 100.

• The U.S. Postal Service can provide you with personalized stamped envelopes in quantities as few as 50, and in either regular or business size. Ask your local Post Office to send you a Personalized Envelope Order Form which explains the options and prices.

• Rootstamps, 6479 White Pine Dr, Lakeside, AZ 85929. Special rubber stamps for genealogists and family reunions. These will really dress up your next mailers. $2 for catalog, refunded with first order. *www.whitemtns.com/~roots/*

• Special reunion stickers for envelopes and mailers. These are designed to get more people to attend your next reunion. See page 128 for details.

CUSTOMIZED CROSSWORD PUZZLES

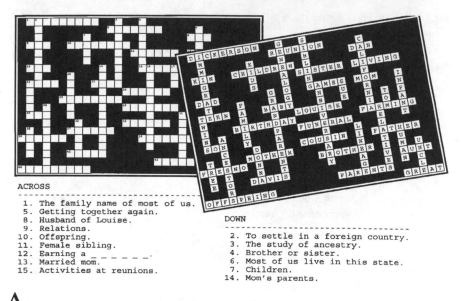

ACROSS
----
1. The family name of most of us.
5. Getting together again.
8. Husband of Louise.
9. Relations.
10. Offspring.
11. Female sibling.
12. Earning a _ _ _ _ _ _.
13. Married mom.
15. Activities at reunions.

DOWN
----
2. To settle in a foreign country.
3. The study of ancestry.
4. Brother or sister.
6. Most of us live in this state.
7. Children.
14. Mom's parents.

A crossword puzzle will really dress up your next newsletter or mailer. Or pass it around at your next reunion—maybe have a contest to see who finishes it first.

Here's how it works:

Send us a list of 50 words relating to your family (please print or type). OR send us a shorter list and we will fill it out to 50 words using common family-oriented words such as "mother," "cousin," "kin," "ancestor," etc.

The puzzle is randomly generated by computer, so some words may not be used (usually only 4–6 are left out). However, you can designate up to 5 words to be used for sure. These words will *not* be left out. Either circle or underline these words on your list. (Remember to print or type the list.)

Then make up a clue for each word. Clues are easier to create than you might think. Short ones are better. Limit of 50 characters per clue (including spaces between words).

We will send you back a blank puzzle, a list of clues, and or course, the solution. Then just paste it into your next newsletter or mailer. Or pass it around at your next reunion.

> **All this for only $19.95. Allow 4 weeks for delivery.**
> **Add $10 for rush orders.**

Send your list of words (50 or as many as you can think of that pertain to your family), a clue for each word, and the check to:

Reunion Research, 3145 Geary Blvd. #14, San Francisco, CA 94118.

Make checks out to "Reunion Research."

IMPORTANT: Include your deadline and phone number.

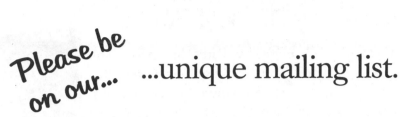

...unique mailing list.

Dear Reunion Planner:

Many businesses offer special discounts and services to reunion planners. Inclusion on this mailing list will help you become better informed which, in turn, will help you create better and more rewarding reunions for your family.

You will not be inundated with mail. You will probably receive anywhere from 5 to 20 pieces of mail per year from businesses that can save you money or can offer you something special for your next reunion. **You can remove yourself from the list at any time.**

Many happy reunions to you.

Tom

Tom Ninkovich

Yes, please include me on a list of family reunion planners.

Name _____

Address _____

City _____ State _____ Zip _____

Approximately how many people attend your reunions? _____

How often do you have reunions? _____

Return this form to:
Reunion Research, 3145 Geary Blvd. #14, San Francisco, CA 94118.

—————— The Book Store ——————

Family Reunion Handbook by Tom Ninkovich. This is the bible for family reunion planners. Over 3000 reunion planners were interviewed to collect material for this book. New 2nd edition, completely revised. $14.95.

Family Associations: Organization and Management by Christine Rose, tells you why and how to go about forming a family association. Includes sample by-laws. New 2nd edition. $12.95.

Directory of Reunion Sites. This annual publication lists reunion sites and accommodations, nationwide. Find out which places cater specifically to family reunions. $3 if purchased alone. Free with any other purchase. No shipping charge.

(Actual size)

We have **envelope stickers** that will definitely get more people to attend your next reunion. Attach to anything you mail out. **They come 10 per card.** Burgundy ink on glossy white paper. Peel-and-stick. Minimum order is 5 cards = $5; 10 cards = $8; 20 cards = $12; 50 cards = $20; 100 cards = $50. No additional shipping charge.

LifeStories is a fun game that gets people talking about their past. Both young and old have such experiences—this is a great game for mixing the ages. The game is designed to build closer relationships among players and to pass on family history. Best of all, everyone wins! For 2 to 8 players, ages 6 to 106. Children over 10 like to play as a group; younger children enjoy the game best when played with adults. $28.95.

Please note: If this is a library book, do *not* tear out this page. Please photocopy it. Pages torn from library books will be returned and not processed.

ORDER FORM

IMPORTANT: If this book is more than 3 years old (see front), write for an updated price before ordering.

Name _____

Address _____

City _____ State ____ Zip _____

ITEM	PRICE	AMOUNT
Family Reunion Handbook	$14.95	$_____
Fun & Games for Family Gatherings ..	12.95	_____
Family Associations: Organization and Management	12.95	_____
Directory of Reunion Sites (no shipping charge)	_____	_____
LifeStories, board game	28.95	_____
Stickers for envelopes .. (no shipping charge) ..	_____	_____
Shipping for one item	2.50	_____
Shipping for each additional item ..	1.50	_____
Sub total		_____
*For Priority Mail add $2 <u>more</u> per item		_____
California residents add current sales tax .		_____
Grand total		_____

Note: We will ship to multiple addresses at no additional charge. Please enclose an address list. If you are buying the book as a gift, we will enclose a gift card if you like. Please show how to make out the card.

*Books will be shipped Book Rate unless Priority is paid for.

Unconditional guarantee: If you are not satisfied with any item for any reason, please return it within 10 days for a full refund.

Make checks payable to: "Reunion Research"
Reunion Research, 3145 Geary Blvd. #14, San Francisco, CA 94118

◆ If you are returning this form for a purchase, check here ☐ to be put on our mailing list (read about our mailing list on page 127). You will *not* be put on the mailing list unless the above box is checked.

ABOUT the AUTHOR

Adrienne Anderson lived on a prairie farm near Calgary, Alberta, Canada until she passed away in February 1996. She worked in the field of Christian education, specializing in creative teaching for all ages. A 25-year interest in tracing her family history led to establishing Genealogy Plus, a traveling and mail-order bookstore (see below). Her avocational interests included travel, reading, cats and her seven grandchildren, not necessarily in that order.

—GENEALOGY PLUS PRICE LIST—

Cat. #		U.S.	Canada
——	*Fun and Games for Family Gatherings*............................	——	$17.95
# 102	Family Group Sheets, 50 for.......................................	$4.50	5.00
	100 for.......................................	8.00	9.00
# 103	Ancestor Charts, 11 x 17, each...	.50	.75
#9001	9 x 12 white envelopes imprinted on front face with family record similar to #102, above. Punched for a 3-ring binder. Suitable for gathering photos, memorabilia. Checklist to indicate items enclosed. 50 for.....................	13.00	15.00

Monographs (brief papers on one topic):

Cat. #		U.S.	Canada
#9003	Obsolete medical terminology..	1.50	2.00
#9004	Obsolete occupations..	1.50	2.00
#9005	What's in a Name? Naming patterns from various cultures.	1.50	2.00
#9006	Titles, ranks and forms of address......................................	1.50	2.00
#9011	Family History Questionnaire. Color coded by life stages: Ancestors, birth, early childhood, etc. An idea file for writing your own story or to use when interviewing relatives. Punched for 3-ring binder..................................	8.00	10.00

Genealogy Plus, Box 69, Langdon, AB, T0J 1X0, Canada
Please make checks payable to Lloyd Anderson
Shipping (U.S. or Canada): Orders under $25, add $2.50. Orders over $25, add $4.

QUANT.	CAT. #	ITEM	PRICE
		SHIPPING	
		TOTAL	

Cross-Reference for Games and Activities

Check the Table of Contents and the Index for other categories. Chapter 1 (Reunion Ideas) and Chapter 9 (Food) are not included below. *The numbers given are game numbers, not page numbers.*

—Level of Activity—

Passive:
#56–59, 62, 65, 70–72, 7, 114, 118, 120–122, 128, 130, 132, 140–149, 151–153, 156–176, 183, Chapter 10, Chapter 11.

Moderately active:
#60, 63–64, 66–69, 73–78, 80–83, 85–86, 93, 96–97, 102–107, 110, 112–113, 117, 123, 129, 131, 150, 154–155, 177–182, 184–191.

Very active:
#79, 84, 88–92, 94–95, 98–101, 108–109, 111, 116, 119, 124–127, 137–139, 155.

Rambunctious:
#133–136

—Other Criteria—

Possible indoor or rainy day activities:
#57–72, 76, 82, 87, 96–97, 102–106, 113–114, 118, 120–122, 128, 130, 132, 137–139, 142–149, 151–154, 156–157, Chapter 7, 172–173, 175–183, 185–191, Chapter 10, Chapter 11.

For all ages (cross-generational) plus noncompetitive:
#70–71, 87, 113–114, 118, 120, 122, 128–130, 132, 140–149, 152–155, 157–158, Chapter 7, 172, 174, 177–185, 187, 189, 207, 210–211, 213–219, 223, 225–228, 230–231.

Fun to watch:
#76, 82, 97, 102–106, 116–119, 123, 140, 142–143, 145, 147, 151, 155, 172, 178–179, 184, 189–190, Chapter 11.

Ice-breakers, mixers:
#57, 62, 71, 152, 174, 208, 210–212, 217–218, 222–223.

Projects:
#57, 155–158, Chapter 7, 172, 209, 221, 224–226.

Statistical games:
#217, 218.

Game and Activity Titles in Alphabetical Order

Adventure Hike (#125)
Ah Stunt (#232)
Animal Blind Man's Bluff (#65)
Animal Cracker Art (#163)
Ante Over (#133)
Ball Tag (#96)
Balloon Catch (#176)
Balloon Relays (#177–182)
Balloon Sculpture (#172)
Balloon Stomp (#188)
Balloon Tournament (#187)
Balloons (#61)
Banana Boats (food) (#201)
Banquet Statistics (#218)
Bean Bag (#78)
Biscuits on a Stick (food) (#203)
Blind Penny Hunt (#67)
Bubble Gum Race (#88)
Capture the Flag (#135)
Cat and Mouse (#75)
Caterpillar (#106)
Chain Tag (#93)
Chariot Relay (#102)
Chinese Tag (#87)
Choosing Teams with Balloons (#173)
Coconut Shell Bird Feeders (#161)
Color Balloon Game (#175)
Color Tag (#95)
Comic Book Characters (#70)
Conversation Piece (#222)
Couple Balloon Stunt (#189)
Cross Tag (#90)
Crows and Cranes (#79)
Diorama (#159)
Dirt Pie (food) (#197)
Double Decker Tug-of-War (#119)
Duck, Duck, Goose (#64)
Earth Ball (#150)
Egg Hunt (#63)
Everybody's Birthday Party (#230)
Face Painting (#58)
Fake Election (#225)
Family Stories (#220)
Farmer in the Dell (#66)
First Name Autograph Hunt (#210)

Flag Relay (#99)
Flashlight Tag (#94)
Flying Dutchman (#80)
Follow the Leader (#60)
Fox and Geese (#84)
Frogs on a Log (food) (#198)
G-Man (#115)
Get Acquainted Autograph Mixer (#211)
Get Acquainted Balloons (#174)
Get Acquainted Yarn Pass (#71)
Good Turn (#130)
Gourmet Hot Dogs (#204)
Great Balloon Battle (#185)
Guided Mystery Walk (#141)
Hare and Hounds Hike (#126)
Hat Fashions (#234)
Hidden People (#113)
Historical Crosses (#215)
Hobo Hike (#124)
Hobo Stew (food) (#205)
Ice Cream Cone Cupcakes (#196)
Ice Melting Contest (#146)
Improbable Headlines (#214)
In and Out the Windows (#73)
Indian Arm Wrestle (#139)
Indian Leg Wrestle (#138)
Irish Scavenger Hunt (#153)
Jello Jiggler Finger Food (#195)
Jellybean Exchange (#62)
Kick the Can (#108)
Kids' Get Acquainted Autograph
    Mixer (#212)
Kite Making (#158)
Knee Walk (#82)
Leaf Prints (#165)
Leap Frog Relay (#100)
Lifesaver Relay (#147)
Lima y Limon (#152)
Link Tag (#91)
Locomotive (#77)
London Bridge (#69)
Marriage Riddle (#216)
Melodrama (#235)
Midnight (#74)
Mini-Musical (#224)

Multi-Channel TV Stunt (#233)

Murder in the Dark (#144)

Musical Animals (#68)

Musical Balloons (#183)

Musical Shamrocks (#154)

Musical Wedding (#229)

My Ship Came In (#143)

Mystery Balls (food) (#192)

Mystery Hike (#127)

Nations (#81)

Nature Walk (#56)

North, South, East, West (#86)

Number One Person (#129)

One Minute Walk (#120)

Organ Donors (#136)

Over-and-Under Leap Frog Relay (#101)

Parachute Game (#149)

Peanut Butter Clay (food) (#199)

Peep Box (#159)

Pinatas (#151)

Pine Cone Bird Feeders (#162)

Play Dough (#57)

Pocket Stew (food) (#206)

Poor Kitty (#72)

Potato Printing (#167)

Press Prints (#166)

Quest (#131)

Relationship Questions (#207)

Rindercella (#231)

Roast Apples (food) (#202)

Rock Painting (#164)

Romances (#219)

Rooster Fight (#137)

Run, Sheep, Run (#109)

S'Mores (food) (#200)

Sand and Seed Pictures (#160)

Sardines (#111)

Sardines in the Dark (#121)

Shadow Tag (#92)

Shaggy Dogs (food) (#193)

Shakespearean Romance (#213)

Silhouettes of Elders (#157)

Sir Walter Raleigh (#116)

Skin the Snake (#103)

Skin the Snake Biathalon (#105)

Skin the Snake Race (#104)

Snow Removal Race (#76)

Sounds (#128)

Spatter Painting (#171)

Splat (#186)

Sponge Painting (#168)

Spoon on a String (#145)

Spot Spy (#132)

Squirt (#117)

Stagecoach (#142)

Statistical Treasure Hunt (#217)

Statues (#83)

Steal the Bacon (#110)

Stilts (#156)

Streets and Alleys (#140)

String Art (#169)

Super Balloon Ball (#191)

Swat (#190)

Swat Tag (#89)

Talent Show (#226)

Tangle (#118)

Tear-a-Mural (#170)

Teddy Bear's Picnic (#59)

Themes for Banquets (#221)

This Land Ain't Your Land (#228)

Three Deep (#85)

Tiger Trap (#112)

Tin Can Bowling (#148)

Toilet Paper Pull (#223)

Tongue Twister Song (#227)

Trail Mix (food) (#194)

Travois Race (#155)

Treasure Hunt (#114)

Tunnel Relay (#98)

Water Balloon Toss (#184)

Water Drop (#123)

Wells-Fargo (#134)

Who Am I Booklets (#209)

Who Am I Sheets (#208)

Wink (#122)

Worm Relay (#107)

Zig-Zag Relay (#97)

INDEX

The Directory
of Reunion Sites

The Best
Places in the U.S.
to have a reunion

- Hotels

  - Motels   - CVBs

    - Resorts   - C of Cs

      - Condos   - Cruises

Dear Reunion Planner:

This unique little booklet should be of great help in finding the right location for your next reunion. These places all have special offers for reunion planners. Call or write them to find out exactly what they are. And please mention that you saw their ad in *The Directory of Reunion Sites*.

Below is an explanation of the terms found in the ads:

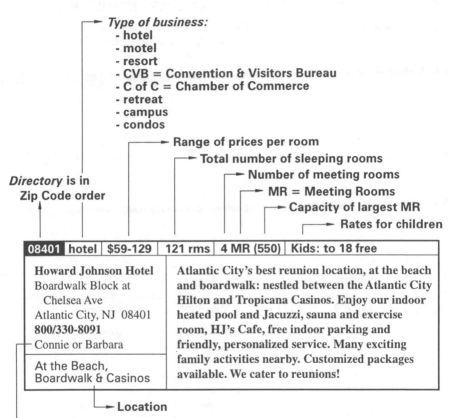

Type of business:
- hotel
- motel
- resort
- CVB = Convention & Visitors Bureau
- C of C = Chamber of Commerce
- retreat
- campus
- condos

→ Range of prices per room
→ Total number of sleeping rooms
→ Number of meeting rooms
→ MR = Meeting Rooms
→ Capacity of largest MR
→ Rates for children

Directory is in
Zip Code order

| 08401 | hotel | $59-129 | 121 rms | 4 MR (550) | Kids: to 18 free |

Howard Johnson Hotel
Boardwalk Block at
   Chelsea Ave
Atlantic City, NJ 08401
800/330-8091
Connie or Barbara

At the Beach,
Boardwalk & Casinos

Atlantic City's best reunion location, at the beach and boardwalk: nestled between the Atlantic City Hilton and Tropicana Casinos. Enjoy our indoor heated pool and Jacuzzi, sauna and exercise room, HJ's Cafe, free indoor parking and friendly, personalized service. Many exciting family activities nearby. Customized packages available. We cater to reunions!

→ Location
→ Person or department to ask for

Abbreviations:
   m = miles, as in "2m" (2 miles)
   < = less than, as in "<16" (less than 16 years old)
   I = Interstate Hwy, as in "I-90" (Interstate 90)
   A/C = air conditioning
   A/V = audio/visual equipment
   pp = per person

Published annually by:
Reunion Research, 3145 Geary Blvd. #14, San Francisco, CA 94118.

| 04614 | cruises | $90-125 | 135 cabins | Free brochure package |

Maine Windjammer Association
PO Box 1144P
Blue Hill, ME 04614
800/807-WIND

Sailing from Camden, Rockport & Rockland

From May to October, our 10 historic ships offer sailing adventures along the coast of Maine. Traditional 6-day packages promise total relaxation, varied ports-of-call, and a beachside lobsterbake. Shorter cruises available. Vessels accommodate 20-40 guests, perfect for groups and family reunions. Let the fresh sea breeze, stars, snug harbors and delicious Downeast cooking whisk you away to a simpler world.

| 05155 | resort | $59-220 | 290 rms | 5 MR (300) | Kids: Special Deals |

Stratton Mountain Resort
RR1, Box 145
Stratton Mountain, VT 05155
800/250-4412

In the southern Green Mountains of Vermont

Vermont's premier 4-season resort, located on 4,000 acres. Skiing, 27-hole golf course, golf school, tennis school, sports center, Kids Kamp, gondola rides, adventure center. Village with shopping, restaurants. Meeting and banquet facilities. Special events year-round. Hotels and condominiums.

| 06905 | hotel | $69-159 | 445 rms | 28 MR (1000) | Kids: Free in parents rm |

Tara Stamford Hotel
2701 Summer St.
Stamford, CT 06905
203/359-1300

1/2m to Downtown, 30m to NYC, 35m to NYC Airports

Five story full-service hotel with spacious guest rooms. Club level, with its own lounge and a variety of suites. 45 minutes from New York City by car or Metro-North commuter railroad. Easy accessibility to I-95 and the Merritt Parkway. Walking distance to a variety of shops, restaurants, movie theatres, and park. Restaurant and lounge in lobby. Free parking for 550 cars.

| 08401 | hotel | $59-129 | 121 rms | 4 MR (550) | Kids: to 18 free |

Howard Johnson Hotel
Boardwalk Block at Chelsea Ave
Atlantic City, NJ 08401
800/330-8091
Connie or Barbara

At the Beach, Boardwalk & Casinos

Atlantic City's best reunion location, at the beach and boardwalk: nestled between the Atlantic City Hilton and Tropicana Casinos. Enjoy our indoor heated pool and Jacuzzi, sauna and exercise room, HJ's Cafe, free indoor parking and friendly, personalized service. Many exciting family activities nearby. Customized packages available. We cater to reunions!

| 08540 | hotel | $89-159 | 348 rms | 12 MR (1000) | Kids: <17 free w/ adult |

Hyatt Regency Princeton
102 Carnegie Center
Princeton, NJ 08540
609/987-1234

40m S. of Newark Airport
40m E. of Philadelphia

Full service hotel featuring a beautiful atrium, keyless security guest room entry, individual voicemail, complimentary in-room iron/ironing board, hair dryer, coffee maker, fully equipped health facility, outdoor tennis & basketball courts, indoor/outdoor pool. Free parking. Near historic Princeton Univ, Sesame Place, Great Adventure, shopping, golf & canoeing.

18360	CVB	$60-125	10,000 rms	Free Reunion Planning Brochure

Pocono Mountains CVB
1004 Main St
Stroudsburg, PA 18360
800/722-9199
Ask for Ellen

http://www.poconos.org
I-80, 2m W of E PA border

2400 acres of mountains, lakes and rivers. Fall foliage, golf & tennis resorts, skiing, family recreation packages. Enjoy white water rafting, NASCAR racing, hiking, biking and entertainment. Free site planning assistance & tours. 4 season resort destination at a convenient travel location for all compass points. Pennsylvania!—Memories last a lifetime.

12564	resort	$70-82	85 rms	10 MR (250)	Kids: see below

Holiday Hills
   Conference Center
2 Lakeside Dr.
Pawling, NY 12564
914/855-1550

Kids: 2-5, 33% adult rate;
6-12, 50% adult rate

Nestled in the foothills of the Berkshires, 70 miles north of Manhattan is Holiday Hills, an extraordinary 500-acre year-round conference center. Accommodations for 175 people in comfortable rooms with private bath, excellent meeting facilities and scenic lakeside dining provide the perfect setting for your next conference or reunion.

23451	hotel	$50-196	107 rms	3 MR (100)	Kids: Free under 18

Dunes Motor Inn
921 Atlantic Ave
Virginia Beach, VA 23451
800/634-0709
888/566-5630
Sara Blackwelder

Totally renovated in 1997. 100% oceanfront hotel has 2 sundecks w/ spas, outdoor heated pool, gym, game room, on-site restaurant, free parking. Each rm contains 2 dble beds, microwave, fridge, coffeemaker. King rms available. Williamsburg/ Busch Gardens only 40 m; Internatnl airport 30 min. Golf, tennis & waterpark only minutes away.

24210	CVB	$30-150	465 rms	Arts, History, and More!

Abingdon CVB
335 Cummings St.
Abingdon, VA 24210
800/435-3440

Interstate 81,
   exit 17

Add history, culture, and romance to your reunion! Chartered in 1778, Abingdon is a Virginia Historic Landmark. Home to the Barter Theatre, State Theatre of Virginia; the William King Regional Arts Center; The Virginia Creeper National Recreation Trail; and much more! Unique and picturesque facilities for reunions. Call and let us help plan your next reunion!

24477	resort	$60-125	37 rms	1 MR (30)	Kids: 5 & under free

Shenandoah Acres Resort
PO Box 300-FR
Stuarts Draft, VA 24477
800/654-1714
Cottage Office

12m from I-81 & I-64
in Staunton, VA

300-acre family resort at the foot of the Blue Ridge Mtns. Sand-bottom swimming lake, game room, horseback riding, mini-golf, tennis, bike rentals, hiking, ball fields. Outdoor BBQ area w/ pavilion. All rooms A/C, many w/ kitchen & fireplace. Campground & camp cabins. Open all year. Skiing, antiques, historical sites, caverns. Blue Ridge Parkway & Skyline Drive nearby.

| 24540 | hotel | $48-90 | 152 rms | 8 MR (150) | Kids: <18 free in parent's rm |

Stratford Inn
2500 Riverside Dr
Danville, VA 24540
800/DANVILLE
804/793-2500
Lynn Ross

S Central VA
  near NC border

Tastefully decorated rooms and suites. Beautiful outdoor pool and spa. Famous restaurant w/ AAA three diamond rating. Exquisite catering in our Ballroom or off-premises. In the heart of Danville, VA, one hour from Triad International Airport, NC, and Raleigh/Durham Airport, NC. At the intersection of Rt. 29 & 58. Convenient to many points of interest.

| 26003 | resort | $69-145 | 212 rms | 15 MR (350) | Kids: 0-3 free; 4-12 half |

Oglebay Resort
Rt. 88 North
Wheeling, WV 26003
800/972-1991
Mindy L. Matheny

4m to downtown,
62m to airport

Unique 1700-acre year-round resort with excellent accommodations and recreational activities. Oglebay is the largest tourist attraction in West Virginia and has been the site of numerous reunions! Choose from 212 guest rooms or one of 48 cottages. On Property: fishing, swimming, 4 golf courses, pedal boating, 7 retail shops, 2 museums, 30-acre zoo, Waddington Gardens and much more!

| 27835 | CVB | Gateway to Eastern North Carolina |

Greenville-Pitt Co. CVB
525 S. Evans St
Greenville, NC 27835
800/537-5564
Contact: Andrew Schmidt

Coastal NC

The Greenville-Pitt County Convention and Visitors Bureau offers a variety of complimentary services designed to make the reunion planner's job easier. Services include accommodation arrangements, meeting and banquet space arrangements, attendance promotion, tour and events coordination, registration assistance and printed name badges.

| 29502 | CVB | $39 up | Free Florence Visitor's Guide |

Florence CVB
PO Box 3093
Florence, SC 29502
800/325-9005

Located at the I-95 & I-20 interchange, halfway between New York and Miami. Historic sites, museums, mini-tours available, shopping, golf, softball, hockey, bowling and tennis. Civic Center with first class meeting facilities.
FLORENCE, SOUTH CAROLINA, IS YOUR REUNION DESTINATION!

| 30303 | hotel | $89-129 | 1068 rms | 39 MR (2100) | Kids: to 18 free |

**The Westin
  Peachtree Plaza**
210 Peachtree St NW
Atlanta, GA 30303
404/589-7737
Craig Hendrick

12m to airport
30m to Stone Mtn.

Landmark hotel in heart of downtown w/ spectacular city views. Tallest hotel in Western Hemisphere. Rooftop revolving restaurant, bar and view. 1 block from Hard Rock Cafe, Planet Hollywood, MARTA Station. 5 blocks to Underground Atlanta, World of Coca-Cola Museum, Centennial Olympic Park, Georgia Dome, CNN. Easy drive to Stone Mtn., M.L. King Memorial, Six Flags, Turner Stadium.

30303	hotel	$59-99	238 rms	2 MR (125)	Kids: 12 & under stay free

Super 8 Hotel & Conference Center
111 Cone St.
Atlanta, GA 30303
Toll Free: 888/524-2400

238 deluxe single and double rooms, 4500 sq. ft. of meeting/banquet space including a ballroom on the top level of the property. Walking distance to tourist attractions, dining, shopping, entertainment, including Hard Rock Cafe and All Star Cafe. Parking available.

32055	motel	$30-45	100 rms	1 MR (35)	Kids: under 18 free

Knights Inn
Rt 13, Box 201
US 90 & I-75
Lake City, FL 32055
904/752-7720

170m to Orlando

Free golf green fees, 27 hole course. Free local calls. Free cable TV including HBO. Pool and shuffle board. Picnic area and barbeque grill. Large parking area for RVs, motor homes and big trucks. Free continental breakfast.

32118	hotel	241 rms	6 MR (450)	Kids: to 18 free w/ parents

Treasure Island Inn
2025 S. Atlantic Ave
Daytona Beach, FL 32118
800/543-5070
Belinda Damm
www.daytonahotels.com

Direct oceanfront

Eleven story beachfront hotel. 241 rooms and hospitality suites, many w/ kitchens. Oceanfront meeting rooms. Large pool deck. 2 swimming pools, 2 whirlpools, multi-tiered sun deck. Free Family Recreation Program. 2 restaurants, lounge, gift shop, game room. Coupon book worth $1000 at local businesses. Free parking. Special reunion recreation/theme parties available.

32301	CVB	$30-150	Attractions for the whole family.

Tallahassee Area CVB
200 W. College Ave
Tallahassee, FL 32301
800/628-2866
Ask for Convention Sales

www.co.leon.fl.us/
visitors/index

Tallahassee is Florida's "Capital" city. Shaping Tallahassee's character are antebellum homes, historic churches, enchanting gardens, nature trails, historic museums, petting zoos and nearby beaches. Often described as "the other Florida," Tallahassee is truly a Florida to explore. Contact our Convention Sales department for details on services offered and upcoming special events.

32407	resort	1054 rms	Kids: Under 12 stay and play free

Paradise Found Resorts & Hotels
11127 Front Beach Rd.
Panama City, FL 32407
800/807-2232

Full-service resorts and hotels to fill any need. All beach properties are oceanfront. Reunion Specialists on-site. Banquet facilities and 5,500 square feet of meeting space. Located on "The World's Most Beautiful Beaches" in Panama City Beach, Florida. Enjoy hospitality "Southern Style."

See display ad.

| 33040 | hotel | $79-149 | 222 rms | 3 MR (570) | Kids: <16 free |

Holiday Inn 3841 N. Roosevelt Blvd Key West, FL 33040 **800/292-7706** Ask for Sales Dept.	Affordable luxury hotel, located at the "gateway" of Key West Florida. 222 newly refurbished, tropically appointed rooms overlooking lush gardens or the Gulf of Mexico. 3 miles from downtown shopping district. On-site beach, water sports shop, and tennis. 6212 sq. ft. of flexible reunion space (small to large). One mile to airport and golf course. Our staff is dedicated to making your reunion a great success.

| 33312 | hotel | $35-69 | 300 rms | 5 MR (250) | Kids: To 12 free; 13+ adult |

Ramada Inn 2275 State Road 84 Ft. Lauderdale, FL 33312 **800/447-7901 ext 500** Ask for Sales Dept. 3m to airport & beaches	The friendliest place for reunions! In the center of all South Florida attractions. 300 spacious air conditioned rooms with cable TV, FREE Showtime, FREE tennis on two courts, two heated pools, volleyball, golf available, 3000 sq. ft. banquet facilities, restaurant, lounge, game room. Minutes from beaches, Las Olas Blvd, great shopping and all pro sports. FREE airport shuttle, FREE parking.

| 35203 | hotel | $75-95 | 147 units | 7 MR (200) | Kids: <17 free w/ parents |

The Tutwiler Hotel 2021 Park Place N. Birmingham, AL 35203 **205/322-2100 ext 1227** Victoria Cabines 4m to airport	Birmingham's historic Four-Star, Four-Diamond hotel centrally located downtown across from Lynn Park. Nearby attractions include Birmingham Museum of Art, Civil Rights Institute, Alabama Sports Hall of Fame, VisionLand, McWane Center & much more. Restaurant on-site, free airport transportation, roll-aways $15 each. The perfect spot for a special, unique reunion.

| 37395 | resort | $34-95 | 52 cottages | 2 MR (75) |

Watts Bar Resort 6767 Watts Bar Hwy. Watts Bar Dam, TN 37395 **800/365-9598** 16m W of I-75, btw. Knox. & Chatt.	Family oriented, with clean, comfortable cottages. A/C, heat, TV, linens, many w/ kitchens, on scenic Watts Bar Lake. Full-service restaurant, children's menu. Swimming & wading pools, hiking trails, tennis courts, shuffleboard, playground. Gift shop. Guest & transient dockage w/ power. Tackle shop w/ live bait, licenses, fishing boat, pontoon & canoe rentals. *www.wattsbarresort.com*

| 38551 | resort | $36 up | Kids: under 5 free |

Cedar Hill Resort 2371 Cedar Hill Rd Celina, TN 38551 **800/872-8393** **931/243-3201** N Central TN	On beautiful Dale Hollow Lake with 620 miles of shoreline to explore. This complete resort in the Cumberland Mtns, offers 31 cottages, 6 motel rooms, 20 houseboats, a swimming pool, a restaurant and marina. Houseboats hold maximum of 12. Excellent fishing, scuba diving and water skiing. Calm waters, no mosquitos, average 82° summer water temperature. Send for 4-color brochure.

40004	CVB	500 rms	Planning assistance available.

Bardstown-Nelson Co. Tourist & Convention Commission 107 E. Stephen Foster Bardstown, KY 40004 **800/638-4877**	Bardstown...where family, heritage and tradition abound. One of America's top 100 towns offers a variety of unique reunion sites, family attractions and southern hospitality. Visit My Old Kentucky Home, Kentucky Railway Museum, and Stephen Foster The Musical or dine on an elegant Dinner Train, tour world famous distilleries and enjoy unique shopping.
35m S. of Louisville	

40004	hotel	$55-69	102 rms	5 MR (300)	Kids: <19 free w/ parents

Holiday Inn Hwy 31E & Bluegrass Pkwy PO Box 520 Bardstown, KY 40004 **502/348-9253** Ask for "Sales"	Our 102 room hotel features affordable accommodations, award winning service, banquet rooms, fitness facility, beautiful outdoor pool & playground, par-3 9-hole golf course, driving range, and miniature golf. Historic Bardstown, one of America's top 100 small towns, is located in central Kentucky and is within 1 hour's drive of many popular family attractions. Packages available.
35m S. of Louisville	

44446	CVB	$45-120	Free planning guide available.

Trumbull County CVB 650 Youngstwn-Warren Rd Niles, OH 44446 **800/672-9555** Contact Jim Mahon	Nestled in the heart of the Old Connecticut Western Reserve, Trumbull County offers a variety of reunion destinations: golf resort, bed/breakfast inns, and major chain properties. Visit Ohio's 2nd largest Amish community, National McKinley Presidential Memorial, basket factory, twenty-three golf courses, and so much more. Call TODAY!!
1/2 way btw Cleveland & Pittsburgh	

44446	hotel	$45-90	100 rms	1 MR (200)	Kids: to 16 free

Park Inn International 1225 Youngstwn-Warren Rd Niles, OH 44446 **330/652-1761** 330/652-8287 Fax	On the Strip—full of activities! Centrally located to serve Warren-Niles-Youngstown. Kitchenettes available. Complimentary continental breakfast. Outdoor pool. Surrounded by attractions, dining & shopping. A/V equip. for rent. RV parking. Children's activities nearby. 180 holes of golf within 15 miles. Rollaways $7 extra. 45 min. to Sea World & Geauga Lake.
10m N of Youngstown, 5m to I-80	

46360	CVB	$35-120	1200 rms	Free Reunion Planner

LaPorte Co. CVB 1503 S. Meer Rd Michigan City, IN 46360 **800/634-2650** Contact Linda Jones	The perfect location to meet in the Midwest! We're on the southern shore of Lake Michigan along the Indiana Dunes National Lakeshore. Charter fishing, riverboat casino, 135-store upscale outlet mall, historic driving tour, and a variety of museums featuring military history, vintage automobiles, and old lighthouses. Let us help you plan your next reunion.
1 hr E of Chicago on I-94 & I-80/90	

60173 | CVB | $60s-80s | 10,000 rms | Chicago's Northwest Suburbs

Greater Woodfield CVB
1375 E Woodfield Rd
  Suite 100
Schaumburg, IL 60173
800/847-4849
Ask for reunion specialist

35m NW of Chicago
10m to O'Hare Airport

Ideal suburban location—host to hundreds of veterans and family reunions annually. 45 hotels from first class to economy to resorts. Rates discounted on many weekends and holidays. Superb shopping at outlet malls and Woodfield Shopping Center—one of the world's largest. Hundreds of nearby attractions, Medieval Times, riverboat gaming, museums galore and more!

60532 | CVB | $59-99 | Chicago's Affordable Alternative

Lisle Illinois CVB
4746 Main St.
Lisle, IL 60532
800/733-9811

Lisle is conveniently located equidistant between downtown Chicago, O'Hare and Midway Airports. At the intersection of I-88, I-355, and I-294, we are in the heart of Chicagoland. Four first class hotels with excellent rates. A wide variety of restaurants and attractions.

61036 | CVB | Let us do the ground work for you.

**Galena/Jo Daviess Co.
Conv. & Visitors Bureau**
720 Park Avenue
Galena, IL 61036
88-GALENA-2
815/777-3557
Susan Michnevitz

NW corner of IL

Head for our hills! Unique blend of history, family fun, scenery, shopping. Camping, RV hookups, B&Bs, hotels, motels, resorts. Golf (miniature too), water park, museums, alpine slide, parks w/ BBQ grills & pavilions, historical sites. Call for free Visitor's Guide & group package details.
Let us help arrange your best reunion yet!!!

61085 | resort | $custom pkgs. | 2 MR (150) | Near historic Galena

**Maple Lane
  Country Resort**
3114 S. Rush Creek Rd.
Stockton, IL 61085
815/947-3773
Rose V. Stout

NW corner of IL,
  Jo Daviess County

Unique scenic country farmland estate. Pool, gazebo, picnic tables, games. Nearby golf, skiing, state parks, antiques, gambling, historic sites, shopping, restaurants. Tour working farm, cheese factory, petting zoo, herb farm, chocolate factory. Horseback riding, hayrides, family fun nights, craft classes, Kookie Camp, murder mystery dinners. Sleeping capacity 50, plus tents/campers. Homecooked meals. Open all year.

61101 | CVB | $49-110 | 3000 rms | Free reunion planning kit

Rockford Area CVB
211 N. Main St.
Rockford, IL 61101
800/521-0849
Ask for Vickie Fogel

60 min W of O'Hare

Illinois' second largest city, on I-90 & I-39 in north central Illinois. A friendly, hassle-free destination with affordable prices that won't blow you away! World-class attractions, too: Anderson Japanese Gardens, Magic Waters, Time Mueseum, Aldeen Golf Course ....plus 7,000 acres of parks and forest preserves. Free parking. O'Hare shuttles.
See display ad.

62220	motel	$29-59	145 rms	3 MR (70)	Kids: to 12 free

Executive Inn
1234 Centreville Ave
Belleville, IL 62220
888/845-1234
Sandy Preston

Southeast corner of
158 & 15

All A/C. Indoor-outdoor pools, full fitness center, picnic areas, lounge & restaurant, guest laundromat, free meeting room & one complimentary room with 10 rooms paid. Roll-away = $5. Next door to convention center. Belleville historic area, apple & strawberry orchards, Lady of Snow Shrine. Cable TV. HBO.
15 miles to St. Louis Arch and Downtown.

64801	CVB	$30-80	1700 rms	Free meeting planner's guide

Joplin CVB
222 W. 3rd St.
Joplin, MO 64801
800/657-2534
Ask for Teresa Gilliam

I-44 & Hwy. 71

Centrally located; Joplin offers an array of indoor and outdoor activities, suitable for all ages. Groups can gather in one of 19 City Parks. Enjoy a round of golf, canoe and fish the streams, walk the trails, shop for antiques, or walk the mall. Visit the Precious Moments Chapel, George Washington Carver's National Monument, Lowell Davis' Red Oak II.

65615	hotels	Branson Missouri Wholesale Reunion Packages

**Branson America's
  Showplace**
PO Box 2290
Branson, MO 65615
800-627-4596
Ask for Reunion Sales

Edgewood Receptive Service has been serving the Ozarks for over 25 years, offering negotiated wholesale reunion packages. Our friendly and professional staff can accommodate all your reunion needs. Accommodations only, meals only, ticketing only. Complete customized packages and motorcoach transportation.

65616	hotel	$49-79	210 rms	5 MR (150)	Kids: to 13 free

Branson Towers Hotel
236 Shephard of the
  Hills Expressway
Branson, MO 65616
800/683-1122
John Johnson

35m to Airport,
Near all attractions

Full catering and meeting space available at reasonable costs. Oversized rooms w/ 2 queen beds. Indoor pool and spa, complimentary continental breakfast & coffee 24-hrs per day. Whippersnapper Restaurant on property. Gift shop, game room, guest laundry. Reunions get great rates and suite upgrades. Nightly ice cream social in the Grand Piano Lobby.

67202	hotel	$49-69	262 rms	11 MR (1200)	Kids: to 18 free

**The Broadview
A Grand Heritage Hotel**
400 W. Douglas
Wichita, KS 67202
800/362-2929
Heather Hartman

Historic hotel built in 1922. Features 262 sleeping rooms and 25,000 sq. ft. of meeting space. Centrally located downtown. Within walking distance of museums, shopping, baseball stadium, ice skating, and river walks along the Arkansas River. Dog track, aviation museum and zoo close by. Complimentary airport shuttle. Call for more information.

75234	hotel	$59-89	380 rms	10 MR (500)	Kids: to 18 free w/ parents

Holiday Inn Select
2645 LBJ Fwy.
Dallas, TX 75234
972/243-3363
Teddi Davis

9m to DFW Airport
5-30m to all major
attractions

Full-service hotel. Indoor/outdoor heated pool. Terrific location for families. Convenient to Galleria, Texas Stadium, Six Flags, Sandy Lake, West End, Downtown, and other area attractions. Free Health Club, parking, and cable TV. Restaurant and Pizza Hut. Children under 12 eat free with parents. Full conference and banquet facilities. Call or write for our free Reunion Planning Guide.

77024	hotel	$49-99	173 rms	5 MR (150)	Kids: Free

Radisson Suite Hotel
10655 Katy Fwy.
Houston, TX 77024
713/461-6000

Next to
Town & Country Mall

Deluxe 2-room suites sleep up to six. Rooms include full American breakfast buffet, refrigerator and bottled water, microwave and popcorn, coffeemaker, hairdryer and 2 TVs. Exercise room and outdoor pool. Nightly hors d'oeuvres in Lobby Lounge with live music. Convenient access to major attractions, dining and shopping. Hospitality suites. Specially designed reunion packages available.

77056	hotel	$ seasonal	449 rms	29 MR (360)

Doubletree Hotel
2001 Post Oak Blvd
Houston, TX 77056
800/222-8733
713/961-9300
Sales Department

Post Oak-Galleria area

Affordable accommodations for the perfect reunion. 24-hour room service, iron, ironing board, hairdryers and coffee makers in all rooms. Outdoor pool, sauna, exercise room and seasonal pool bar. Attractions include Galleria shopping, Astro World, Water World, LB Johnson Space Center and Museum of Fine Arts.

77090	hotel	$49-129	250 rms	4 MR (75)	Kids: <16 free

Lexington Hotel
16410 N. Fwy. 45
Houston, TX 77090
281/821-1000

Affordable all-suite property featuring spacious studios, one- and two-bedroom suites. Located two miles from IAH Airport, the Lexington Suites also has a heated swimming pool, complimentary breakfast, and easy access to every major freeway. Area attractions include fine cuisine, night life, shopping, Splashtown USA, and Sam Houston Raceway Park.

78216	hotels	$49-119	9 locations/meeting facilities available

The Drury Hotels
  of San Antonio
91 NE Loop 410
San Antonio, TX 78216
210/341-0774
210/341-8244 fax
Ask for Irene Lodge

Locations are in "Central" San Antonio. All hotels offer free continental breakfast, free local calls, free airport shuttle (airport locations only), outdoor swimming pools, free cable TV with one premium movie channel. Suites and auto rentals available at most locations. 100% satisfaction guaranteed. Children under 18 stay free in parents' room. Close proximity to fine restaurants and shopping malls.

78627 | CVB | $40-80 | 295 rms | Free Reunion Planner

Georgetown CVB
PO Box 409
Georgetown, TX 78627
800/436-8696
www.georgetown.org
juliemus@gte.net

25m N of Austin

Halfway between Dallas and San Antonio on Interstate 35, Georgetown is the gateway to the Hill Country. Our charming community is a relaxing getaway for the whole family. Families can enjoy a picnic under old Cyprus trees in San Gabriel Park or a catered meal at one of our meeting facilities. Ask about free games to rent for all ages.

79761 | CVB | $30-85 | 1900 rms | Reunion information available

Odessa CVB
700 N. Grant #200
Odessa, TX 79761
800/780-HOST
915/333-7871

Between El Paso &
Ft. Worth on I-20

Odessa, Texas. A city of contrasts! Professional hockey, Water Wonderland, great shopping, entertainment, and one-of-a-kind museums such as the Confederate Air Force Museum and the Presidential Museum. Major hotel chains with ample convention space. Easily accessible via Midland International Airport. Serviced by Interstate 20 and Highway 385. RV hookups available for any size group.

80424 | resort | $90-250 | Hotel rooms, condominiums, & townhouses

**The Village at
  Breckenridge,
  A Wyndam Resort**
PO Box 8329
Breckenridge, CO 80424
800/332-0424 Call Jim Born

75m W of Denver

The best location in Breckenridge, on Main Street adjacent to the mountains. Activities for both young and old include: horseback riding, golf, biking, hiking, fishing, jeep tours to ghost towns, historic train rides, gold panning, alpine slides, campfire cook-outs and more. Film, art and music festivals occur throughout the summer months. Never a dull moment!

80446 | resort | $59-149 | 342 rms | 16 MR (300) | Kids: 17 & under free

Inn at Silver Creek
PO Box 4222
Silver Creek, CO 80446
800/926-4386 (press 2)
Ask for Charles

90 min NW of Denver
on Hwy 40

Under one roof, our hotel offers a variety of affordable family accommodations featuring kitchenettes, fireplaces, patios, newly remodeled athletic club w/ heated outdoor pool, sundeck, 4 hot tubs, sauna, weight room, tennis courts, restaurant and bar, giftshop. Centrally located between Rocky Mountain National Park and Winter Park Resort. Lots of activities!! Call Today!

80482 | condos | $70-400 | 115 units | 2 MR (50) | The Perfect Location

Beaver Village Condos
PO Box 349
50 Village Dr
Winter Park, CO 80482
800/824-8438
Ask for Group Dept.

3 blks frm Downtown
  Winter Park

Home away from home in a secluded forest property. Deluxe 1, 2, and 3 bedroom condominiums with fully equipped kitchens and fireplaces. Clubhouse with heated indoor pool, sauna, 3 hot tubs, and meeting room with catering kitchen. Only 1.5 miles to Winter Park Resort for summer and winter fun.

80482	resort	$69-559	130 rms	5 MR (150)	Kids: free in unit w/ adults

Iron Horse Resort PO Box 1286 Winter Park, CO 80482 **800/621-8190** Group Sales Winter Park's premier resort & conf. center	Winter Park's only ski-in/ski-out resort & conference center. Iron Horse features condominium accommodations w/ full hotel services. Fully equipped units from studios to 2 bdrm 3 bath suites. Restaurant & lounge, outdoor swimming pool, 4 hot tubs, exercise rm, secluded group picnic area, free local shuttle. A luxury resort at affordable prices. Special seasonal group value packages.

80482	condos	290 rms	1 MR (55)	Kids: Free w/ paying adult

Winter Park Adventures PO Box 66 Winter Park, CO 80482 **800/832-7830** 70m NW of Denver	Reunion specialists offering 30 properties, varied amenities and price ranges. Summer activities include Rocky Mountain National Park, golfing, mountain biking, river rafting, horseback riding, fishing, hiking, alpine slide, rodeos, boating and more. Winters offer world class downhill skiing, snowmobiling, ice skating, sleigh rides. Call for package details.

80903	CVB	$25-300	9700 rms	Free Visitor Guide

Colorado Springs CVB 104 S. Cascade Ave #104 Colorado Springs, CO 80903 **800/888-4748 Ext 138** *See our display ad.*	Located at the foot of famous Pikes Peak, Colorado Springs offers magnificent mountain scenery and a delightful, seasonal climate. Excellent accommodations are available for every taste and budget. Unique, exciting attractions and recreational opportunities offer every visitor an unforgettable adventure....from the Garden of the Gods and Air Force Academy to gaming in Cripple Creek.

87110	hotel	$59-99	173 rms	4 MR (225)	Kids: To 17 free

**Best Western
  Winrock Inn**
18 Winrock Center NE
Albuquerque, NM
  87110
800/866-5252
Julie Hasty
8m fm airport on I-40
	Located in Uptown Entertainment District. Hotel w/ beautiful lagoon w/ ducks & fish. Adjacent to mall, movie theaters, & many restaurants. Free full hot breakfast buffet included in rate. Outdoor heated pool. Banquet rms w/ catering. Lots of attractions nearby: fairgrounds, Atomic Museum, Sandia Tramway, golf courses, Old Town, zoo, aquarium. Free parking. 1 comp guest room per 15 paid.

87710	C of C	Free 4-color visitors guide.

Angel Fire Chamber of Commerce PO Box 547 Angel Fire, NM 87710 **800/446-8117** 25m E of Taos, NM, on Hwy 434	A premier family ski and golf resort area high in the Sangre de Cristo mountains of northern New Mexico. Hotels, condos, houses for rent. Meeting rooms, picnic areas, catered parties. Mountain biking, horseback riding, hiking, fishing & golf. In winter: skiing, snowmobiling, sleigh rides and more. www.angelfirenm.com E-mail: chambr@angelfirenm.com

90602	hotel	$69-89	202 rms	8 MR (350)	Kids: to 18 free w/ parents

Whittier Hilton
7320 Greenleaf Ave
Whittier, CA 90206
562/945-8511
Tatiana Paton

Off I-605, between I-10 and I-5

Centrally located between all major Los Angeles airports and freeways, the AAA, 3 Diamond rated Whittier Hilton provides an ideal hub for business and leisure travelers visiting Los Angeles and Orange Counties. 150 unique shops, restaurants and theaters. Pool, spa and fitness center. 30 minutes from Disneyland and Knotts Berry Farm. 30 minutes from downtown Los Angeles.

92101	hotel	$89-150	280 rms	23 MR (950)	Kids: to 12 free

U.S. Grant Hotel
326 Broadway
San Diego, CA 92101
800/237-5029
Ask for Group Sales

Located in Downtown San Diego

Historic hotel across frm Horton Plaza (outdoor mall w/ 135+ stores). Walking distance to GasLamp Quarters w/ 75+ restaurants, Seaport Village, San Diego Bay & Children's Museum. Minutes to world famous Zoo and SeaWorld. Complimentary hospitality suite & airport transp. 2 restaurants, Bruegger's Bagels & Chandler's Gift Shop. Recipient of Mobil Four Star & AAA Four Diamond awards.

92106	hotel	$72-115	237 rms	3 MR (160)	Kids: <19 free w/ adult

Holiday Inn
  San Diego Bayside
4875 N. Harbor Dr.
San Diego, CA 92106
800/662-8899
Ask for Sales Dept.

See our display ad.

Beautiful bayside location offering renovated and spacious guest rooms w/ refrigerators, coffee, hairdryers, pay-per-view movies and free HBO. Amenities include a large heated pool and spa, tropical courtyard w/ billiards and ping-pong, a 9-hole putting course and exercise room. Reunions receive a complimentary hospitality suite. Water-view banquet rms & poolside courtyard are available. Free parking.

92614	hotel	$96-112	293 rms	5 MR (150)	Kids: 12 & under free

Embassy Suites Hotel
2120 Main St
Irvine, CA 92614
714/553-8332
Melissa Gordon

1/2m to 405/55
1/2m to Airport

All-suite hotel. Private bedrooms. Complimentary full cooked-to-order breakfast. Complimentary beverages for 2 hours nightly. Refrigerator, 2 TVs, free cable/movie channel, coffee maker, hair dryer, ironing board/iron. Indoor pool, whirlpool, sauna/ fitness center. Meeting space capacity to 150. Restaurant/catering.

93463	resort	$335/415	73 rms	6 MR (150)	Kids:<2 free; 3-5 $40; 6+ $65

The Alisal Guest Ranch
  and Resort
1054 Alisal Rd
Solvang, CA 93463
800/425-4725, Ext 264
Dianne Calderon, DOS

40m N of Santa Barbara, 35m to S.B. Airport

Resort-bungalows with wood burning fireplaces. Modified American Plan includes breakfast/dinner. Activities available: golf (2, 18-hole championship courses), tennis, horseback riding, fishing and boating on private lake, children's programs. Round-up Vacation Package (RUV) includes all activities for 2 during certain times of the year. *E-mail:* sales@alisal.com *Internet:* www.alisal.com

95112	hotel	$89-229	515 units	14 MR (600)	Kids: Under 18 free

Hyatt San Jose	A full-service hotel on 18 acres in the heart of Silicon
1740 N. First St.	Valley. Lush landscaped gardens w/ gazebos, ponds,
San Jose, CA 95112	outdoor swimming pool w/ Jacuzzi. Just 1 mile from
408/793-3976	San Jose International Airport. 21,000 sq. ft. of banquet
Michael Robasciotti	space. An ideal environment for your next family or
	class reunion. Newly renovated guestrooms. Complete
1m from San Jose Airport	amenity package includes computer, fax, printer, and
	Net accessibility. Groups to 1000. Free parking.

95354	CVB	$35-120	1500 rms	Come visit Castle Air Museum

Modesto Convention	Have the best of ALL worlds! Meet in a warm &
& Visitors Bureau	welcoming city in the center of California! Enjoy
1114 "J" St	attractions from Hershey's Chocolate to Yosemite
Modesto, CA 95354	Nat'l. Park and San Francisco. Pan for gold in
800/266-4282	the nearby Gold Country, tour the St. Stan's
Phyllis Rabusin	Brewery and Delicato Vineyards. Visit nearby
	Castle Air Museum. Free reunion services. Great
Central Valley of Calif.	hotel packages!

95451	resort	$25-150	8 cabins	1 MR (75)	Kids: under 5 free

Edgewater Resort	Guaranteed the best full-service campground on
6420 Soda Bay Rd	the 100-mile shoreline of Clear Lake. 8 cabins, 61
Kelseyville, CA 95451	RV/camping sites. Group BBQ patio, commercial
800/396-6224	kitchen & clubhouse. Pool, beach, pier, dock, boat
Sandra West	launch/rentals, laundry, pets OK. Activities: lawn
	or pool volleyball, horseshoes, ping-pong, game-
2.5 hr N of San Francisco	room, unlimited watersports & fishing. Nearby
2 hr W of Sacramento	golf and hiking. Ask about Reunion Specials.

96740	resort	$68-100	530 rms	12 MR (1200)	Kids: <18 free

Kona Surf Resort	530 rm oceanfront hotel, considered one of the
and Country Club	best-valued resorts on the Big Island. Next to
78-128 Ehukai St	Keauhou Bay, near Kailua-Kona. Salt water &
Kailua-Kona, HI 96740	fresh water swimming pools, 36-hole golf course,
800/932-9466	tennis, volleyball, shuffleboard, free Polynesian
www.ilhawaii.net/konasurf	shows. Rooms are large, have magnificent views,
Ask for "Sales"	free coffee & refrigerators. In Honolulu, see sister
16m to Airport	property, Hawaiian Waikiki Beach Hotel.

97528	CVB	$35-125	Group Rates—Great Fun—Good Company

Grants Pass V&CB	1200 rooms to choose from. We maintain a close
PO Box 1787	relationship with local lodging, restaurants, and
Grants Pass, OR 97528	attractions. Located in the middle of an outdoor
541/476-5510	recreation "mecca" with tons of activities for every
Convention Sales	member of your group. Grants Pass, Oregon, is
	"Where the Rogue River runs."
SW Oregon	

Other Hotels and Agencies that Offer Reunion Accommodations.

Listed in Zip Code order.

Best Western Black Swan Inn, Route 20, Lee, MA 01238, **800/876-7926**

Radisson Hotel, 11 Beaver St, Milford, MA 01757, **508/478-7010**

Hilton at Dedham Place, 25 Allied Dr, Dedham, MA 02026, **617/329-7900**

Heritage Inn Conference Resort, Heritage Rd, Southbury, CT 06488

Town House Motel, 351 Franklin St, Hightstown, NJ 08520, **800/922-0622, x405**

Ramada Inn, 195 Route 18 South, E. Brunswick, NJ 08816, **908/828-6900**

Hofstra University, 111 Student Center, Hempstead, NY 11550, **516/463-5067**

Gavin's Golden Hill Resort, PO Box 6, E Durham, NY 12423, **800/272-4591**

Watson Homestead Retreat, 9620 Dry Run Rd, Painted Post, NY 14870, **800/962-8040**

Lehigh Valley CVB, 2200 Avenue A, Bethlehem, PA 18017, **800/747-0561**

Pocono Mountains CVB, 1004 Main St, Stroudsburg, PA 18360, **800/722-9199**

Wyndam Bristol Hotel, 2430 Pennsylvania Ave NW, Wash DC 20037, **202/955-6400**

Hyatt Dulles, 2300 Dulles Corner Blvd, Herndon, VA 22071, **703/713-1234**

Quality Inn/Shenandoah Valley, PO Box 100, New Market, VA 22844, **540/740-3141**

Atlanta's DeKalb CVB, 750 Commerce Dr #200, Decatur, GA 30030, **800/999-6055, x7581**

Days Inn, 60 S. Beachview Dr, Jekyll Island, GA 31527, **888/635-3003**

Marina Hotel & Conf. Center, 530 N Palmetto Ave, Sanford, FL 32771, **800/290-1910**

The Ritz Plaza, 1701 Collins Ave, Miami Beach, FL 33139, **305/534-3500**

The Shore Club, 1901 Collins Ave, Miami Beach, FL 33139, **800/327-8330**

Ramada Resort, 6701 Collins Ave, Miami Beach, FL 33141, **305/865-8511**

Embassy Suites, 3974 NW South River Dr, Miami, FL 33142, **800/772-3787, x370**

Marriott Hotel, 6650 N. Andrews Ave, Ft. Lauderdale, FL 33309, **954/771-0440, x6621**

Embassy Suites, 1100 SE 17th St, Ft Lauderdale, FL 33316, **800/854-6146**

Holiday Inn, 6600 S. Tamiami Trl., Sarasota, FL 34231, **941/924-4900**

Hampton Inn, 5995 Cattleridge Rd, Sarasota, FL 34232, **941/371-1900**

Fountain Park Resort Hotel, 5150 West U.S. 192, Kissimmee, FL 34746, **800/672-9601**

The Ohio State Park Resorts, Rt 2, PO Box 7, Cambridge, OH 43725, **800/990-9020**

Holiday Inn Lakeside, 1111 Lakeside Ave, Cleveland, OH 44114, **216/241-5100**

Oak Cove Resort, 58881 46th St, Lawrence, MI 49064, **616/674-8228**

Hotel Fort Des Moines, 1000 Walnut, Des Moines, IA 50309, **800/532-1466**

Racine Marriott Hotel, 7111 Washington Ave, Racine, WI 53406, **414/886-6100**

Nelson's Resort, 7632 Nelson Rd, Crane Lake, MN 55725, **800/433-0743**

Hotel Alex Johnson, 523 6th St, Rapid City, SD 57701, **800/888-ALEX (2539)**

Days Inn O'Hare S., 3801 N Mannheim Rd, Schiller Park, IL 60176, **847/678-0670**

Hampton Inn, 1087 E. Diehl Rd, Naperville, IL 60563, **630/505-1400, 630/505-1416**

Executive Inn, 1234 Centreville Ave, Belleville, IL 62220, **888/845-1234**

Mt. Vernon CVB, 200 Potomac Blvd, Mt. Vernon, IL 62864, **800/252-5464**

Van Buren C of C, PO Box 356, Van Buren, MO 63965, **800/692-7582**

Thousand Hills Golf Resort, 245 S. Wildwood Dr, Branson, MO 65616, **800/697-9472**

Best Western Inn of the Ozarks, PO Box 431, Eureka Springs, AR 72632, **800/552-3785**

Marriott Hotel, 3233 Northwest Expwy, Oklahoma City, OK 73112, **405/879-7014**

La Grange Area C of C, 171 S. Main, La Grange, TX 78945, **800/LAGRANG**

Wildwood Suites, PO Box 565, 120 Sawmill Rd, Breckenridge, CO 80424, **800/866-0300**

B/W Le Baron Hotel, 314 W Bijou St, Colo. Springs, CO 80905, **800/477-8610, x448**

Hampton Inn, Gold Dust & Scottsdale Rd, Scottsdale, AZ 85253, **602/443-3233**

Ramada Plaza Hotel, 1600 South 52, Tempe, AZ 85281, **800/346-3049, 602/967-6600**

Best Western Executive Inn, 333 W Drachman, Tucson, AZ 85705, **800/255-3371**

Carlsbad C of C, PO Box 910, Carlsbad, NM 88221, **800/221-1224**

Quality Hotel, 5249 W Century Blvd, Los Angeles, CA 90045, **310/645-2200, x1321**

Carson Hilton Inn, 2 Civic Plaza Dr, Carson, CA 90745, **310/830-9200, x107**

La Quinta Resort and Club, 49-499 Eisenhower Dr, La Quinta, CA 92253, **800/598-3828**

Riverside CVB, 3443 Orange St, Riverside, CA 92501, **909/222-4700**

Radisson Miyako Hotel, 1625 Post St, San Francisco, CA 94115, **800/533-4557**

Cupertino Inn, 10889 N. DeAnza Blvd, Cupertino, CA 95014, **800/222-4828**

Bell Haven Resort, 3415 White Oak Way, Kelseyville, CA 95451, **707/279-4329**

Rocky Point Resort, 3894 Lakeshore Blvd, Lakeport, CA 95453, **707/263-4673**

Sandy Bar Ranch, PO Box 347, Ishi Pishi Rd, Orleans, CA 95556, **916/627-3379**

Inn by the Lake, 3300 Lake Tahoe Blvd, S. Lake Tahoe, CA 96150, **800/877-1466**